*Phenomenology and Science
in Contemporary European Thought*

IN CONTEMPORARY

Phenomenology and Science

EUROPEAN THOUGHT

Anna-Teresa Tymieniecka

with a Foreword by I. M. Bochenski

FARRAR, STRAUS AND CUDAHY

I wish to express my thanks, as this book is going to press, to those who have helped me in its preparation. Mr. Michael Dummitt generously read the first draft and helped me immeasurably with my style. Professor S. C. Pepper's and Dr. Ludwig Lefebre's kind interest was an important stimulus in the early stages of this work. To Professor Lelland Rather, M.D., I am indebted for invaluable comment and criticism. Mr. Cecil Hemley, my editor, suggested many improvements. My husband, Hendrik Houthakker, knows how much I owe him for his constant encouragement of my endeavors.

Anna-Teresa Tymieniecka

Belmont, Mass.
March, 1961

FOREWORD

"Philosophy" has always been an ambiguous term, more so perhaps in English than in some other languages; but it has not been commonly realized, I think, that nowadays it has a new ambiguity, of a curiously geographical sort. In fact, when we talk about philosophy, it is necessary to make clear to what large geographical group of philosophers we are referring. Roughly speaking there are three such groups: the Continental European, the Anglo-American, and the Soviet. It is not implied by this that all countries and only those comprehended under the above terms are addicted to the said sort of philosophy. For example, the so-called "Continental philosophy" is not the main trend in Poland or Finland, while it seems to be much cultivated in South America. Yet there *are* three sorts of philosophy and they are in some way geographically distributed in our contemporary world.

What are the differences between them? There is, of course, a different approach to the subject. Many historians think also that the very subject, or at least the central problems of those three philosophies are different. Thus it has been suggested that Anglo-American philosophy is centered on science, while Continental philosophy is mostly interested in man. This is, at least partially, true, yet one feels that the classes of problems treated in different groups are not necessarily exclusive. Several instances could be quoted to confirm this view. Just to name one, while Anglo-American philosophers are notoriously interested in the problem of universals, we find quite similar interests and sometimes— as in Merleau-Ponty—ample studies among the partisans of Continental "existentialism." Indeed, I have argued elsewhere that the different schools are complementary rather than competitive.

However, the representatives of different currents of thought are not on speaking terms. They will, at best, listen politely to their colleagues from another camp, but hardly come down to a discussion. They practically never read books proceeding from the opposite group or groups. There is no dialogue between them.

This, I venture to submit, is unfortunate. One need not admit that the other philosopher's method and approach are correct in order to recognize that one could perhaps learn something from him. Let me be quite explicit. I believe that the Soviet dogmatic approach to philosophical problems is completely preposterous and that its fundamental method rests upon a heap of superstition. Yet this does not necessarily prevent the Soviet thinkers from sometimes coming up with interesting thoughts.

But if this is even true from that strange sort of philosophy we call "Soviet," how much more should we say the same when we consider the mutual relations of Anglo-American and Continental thought! There, I feel, we have at least one common assumption, namely, that a philosopher has to use experience and reason alone, that he is not allowed to base his speculation on any authority or mythology. One may be cool to the phenomenological approach and yet find it difficult to deny—if one has ever read the *Logische Unter-suchungen*—that there is much to be said for Husserl and his school, if for no other reason than that he stated so many problems that interest also the analytical philosopher. And if anybody would like to deny it, may I remind him that the whole program of studies on formal logic, syntax, semantics, and many other things have been developed by him, that his thoughts about the meaning of words, the *Bedeutungs-kategorien* and so on appear even to the most hard-boiled analyst as valuable contributions to *his own* line of thought.

That is why a man who, like the undersigned, has been addicted during practically his whole life to the analytical (i.e., Anglo-American as I have called it) type of thinking can, and I think should, welcome Dr. Tymieniecka's book. Her aim is precisely to explain the phenomenological approach in various disciplines to those who are not only not committed, but indeed quite foreign to it. She introduces this approach in a manner intermediary between the highly speculative formulations of its leading proponents and the sober, matter-of-fact attitude of the Anglo-American reader.

She brings to this task an intimate acquaintance with the philosophical foundations of phenomenology, a deep interest in the influence which it has exercised on a variety of disciplines, and a sympathetic understanding of the difficulties faced by those who approach phenomenology from an analytical background. The plan of her book reflects these concerns. In each of its three chapters there are three parts. The first states the theme as presented by Husserl, Jaspers, and Heidegger respectively. The second shows how the new philosophical ideas discussed in the first part have been instrumental in revolutionizing scientific inquiry. The third part gives a philosophical interpretation of the scientific results attained.

By thus putting developments in particular sciences in the center of attention, she achieves three things. Without engaging in polemics she meets head-on one of the common objections to phenomenology, namely, that it is too vague and speculative to be relevant to more concrete researches. No less important, she shows how Husserl's original thoughts have gradually been adapted to the requirements of different subject matters. Thirdly, she makes it clear how, despite this differentiation, there is a philosophical unity underlying much of contemporary European scientific endeavor. She shows this methodological unity embodied in the concept of the many-layered structure. This book does not claim to give new phenomenological insights, but it makes a contribution to philosophy by tracing—apparently for the first time—the development of the phenomenological method in a variety of specialized fields. It attempts to show how phenomenology outlines a scheme of universal inquiry in which empirical and deductive methods find their proper place and can cooperate toward a complete world view. It is therefore of interest not only to novices but also to those who are already familiar with phenomenology.

Viewed from the standpoint of strict modern analysis, this book may at first appear strange. Nothing in it recalls those highly technical discussions on scientific method, induction and probability, on deductive systems and decision problems, and many other subjects of which other analytical books on science are full. And yet it is a book that deals with science, the same great phenomenon which stands there as a reality before the philosopher's eye. The more we penetrate its inner structure, the harder it appears to understand. If I may use a pictorial metaphor, science is like a high mountain in which we are trying to drill a gallery in order to know what is inside it. The analytical school resembles a team of men, armed with highly refined tools, at work in one such gallery. But there might be other men working with other tools, perhaps as refined, if very different, from another side. Dr. Tymieniecka conveys to us the attitude of this other team of workers.

I am not yet sure in how far these workers are successful, even though Dr. Tymieniecka has done much to clarify the structure and the use of their tools. I am writing these pages during the Stanford Congress of Logic and Methodology, from the middle of the analytical team, as it were. My ears are full of the roar of that powerful drilling machine which is contemporary mathematical logic, and yet I feel that we have not the right to be bigoted and dogmatic about science. If one would ask why, I would suggest that this is because of the incredible complication of nature and of human knowledge. This is perhaps one point on which the philosopher *has* the right to be dogmatic: Reality is tremendously complex, and every simple scheme which reduces it, or our ways of knowing it, to a single principle or method, must be *a priori* wrong. This does not entail that every approach other than ours is correct. But it *may* be so. And in order to know if it is correct, one must know it. There is only one way to decide scientifically and this begins with a serious attempt to understand what there is. The *tolle lege* of St. Augustine appears once more as a universal basic rule of scientific method.

I.M. BOCHENSKI

Stanford, California
September 1, 1960

CONTENTS

INTRODUCTION

Philosophy and science determine the main tendencies of the twentieth century. As ideology and technology (in other words, in their popular forms), they have been seen as the causes of what is considered to be the devastating dehumanization of man. But ideology and technology are not the only expressions of modern science. Indeed, a particular form of science has arisen which shows signs of developing into a new Renaissance.

Today, on the Continent, the rationales of many disciplines have undergone profound change, and during two decades the new spirit that has been growing since the turn of the century has flowered into what can be considered a new cultural era. The ideas underlying the new attitudes have already often been described and interpreted, but it is one thing to report what has been going on and another to see its full significance. This book seeks to make at least a beginning toward such an understanding by attempting to penetrate to the deeper roots of this world view and by so doing arrive at some conclusions concerning its permanent significance. In other words, our aim is not to give yet another commentary on the new humanistic spirit in Continental thought, nor do we wish to describe its social manifestations. Our aim is rather to examine as objectively as possible the interrelationships of science and philosophy which have made the new movement possible.

We have taken as our point of focus the very significant work done in phenomenology in this century. It should be pointed out that interest in the phenomenological techniques as applied to both philosophic and scientific investigation has been growing at a rapid pace. One thing, however, should be kept in mind. "Science" (German *Wissenschaft*), as used here, does not mean necessarily merely the experimental sciences, its customary meaning in English, but also signifies both the natural sciences (*Naturwissenschaften*) and the humanities (*Geisteswissenschaften*). That this is not a mere linguistic convention will be evident when the historical relations of philosophy and science and the aim and originality of the phenomenological approach are discussed below.

The variety of disparate disciplines and doctrines claiming allegiance to the phenomenological method is considerable and still growing, but one of our theses is that there is no *one* phenomenological method. The basic foundation of the phenomenological orientation, which consists of elements common to all its variants, must be distinguished from the various phenomenological techniques applied to special subject matters. By applying the basic phenomenological principles many sciences were revolutionized, new sciences developed, and new dimensions and original conclusions concerning man and the world established. In this manner scholarship from diverse areas has converged to shape a consistent philosophical outlook. Thus the articulated constituents of this outlook are not results of pure philosophical speculation, and any attempt to explain them would be grossly distorted if it were not recognized that they are conditioned by the nature of the several special fields.

The best way to delineate the new Humanism is to examine the relations between philosophy and science as these figure in three dominant issues in contemporary Continental thought: *the apodictic foundation of knowledge, knowledge of others,* and *the nature of the world.* This explains the organization of the book as a series of interpretations of concrete scientific researches. It is hoped that these researches will be seen as variants of the basic theme, and that they will ultimately synthesize into a philosophical conception of man's nature and his role in the world, a conception which underlies much of Continental philosophy, science, art, and life.

Our purpose is to develop a theme rather than to write a history. Occasionally it will be convenient to include discussion of thinkers who are not generally considered of the first rank and to omit others who would have a prominent place in a more conventional historical survey. Our choice of figures and themes will be justified if the reader gains some insight into the spirit of contemporary Continental philosophy and science.

Philosophy and science emerged as one discipline. However, there soon followed the realization of the necessity for a distinction between the search for ultimate principles and the search for immediate causes. Since then, although they were usually intermingled and until recently not sharply distinguished, the history of philosophy and science has been charged with constant tension. Their separation was of paramount importance for the progress of both: each has developed by redefining its methods and objectives while using the other as a model, critic, guide, or source of information.

History has amply shown the futility of either dissociating philosophy and science entirely or of replacing one with the other. True, the overwhelming progress achieved by the natural sciences in the nineteenth century, when they claimed their exclusive domains and defined their specific objectives, led them to break from the conceptual framework they had hitherto shared with philosophy. Their divorce from philosophy seemed final. This apparent divorce had two significant and related consequences which deeply marked the thought of the late nineteenth century.

First, the startling practical results made possible by the natural sciences led to the acceptance of their method as the only fit standard for truly scientific endeavor. Fields of scholarship which had enjoyed the status of scientific enterprises could no longer validate their claim. This division between the sciences and other cognitive domains was made without the least attempt to discover whether there are methods other than the "scientific" which might satisfy the criteria of precision and verifiability by means of which the scientific method had gained its prestige. Nor was it even suggested that results obtained in the "pseudo-scientific" inquiries might possibly be of some utility, perhaps as vital to man's existence as the technological wonders supplied by science. The prestige of being "scientific," based upon what had been accomplished in a limited domain, accrued exclusively to the benefit of inquiries which aped the techniques of the physical sciences.

Second, a strong reductionist attitude stemming from scientific premises gradually infiltrated all fields of intellectual activity. The great appeal of Darwin's and Spencer's theories of biological and social evolution lay in their outline of a process of positive investigation which rested on the assumption that complex forms of life could be explained by their origins in simpler forms. It needed only one more short step to transfer this process uncritically to other types of human activities. Complex cultural configurations, for example, were supposed to be explained when they were reduced to particular social conditions. The social phenomena could be further reduced to economic and psychological factors—thus the dream of ultimate explanation in strictly scientific, physical terms. This reductionist attitude, so congenial to the new idea of science, pervaded all thought at the end of the nineteenth century and the beginning of the twentieth, and in Anglo-American thought continues to predominate.

Philosophy's claim to be a science, or at least scientific, had suddenly become problematic. If the several natural sciences embrace all truly legitimate inquiries and if philosophy is construed in the traditional manner, there seems to be no properly philosophical task; and indeed abstract thought, lacking empirical verification, appears to be a positive hindrance to legitimate research. How could philosophy maintain its respectability in the face of acknowledged sciences which were methodical, well confirmed, and practically efficacious? The traditional philosophical aim of *founding* and *unifying* the sciences also seemed misguided as the sciences were extended to incorporate ever vaster domains and even the search for a basic unity underlying their departmental researches seemed to belong no more to philosophy.

Contemporary European philosophy, reaffirming the mutual obligations of philosophy and science, arose at the beginning of the twentieth century in response to the challenge laid down by the nineteenth-century conception of modern science. The work of Husserl and Scheler provided the phenomenological cornerstone of the new philosophical edifice. The task which phenomenology set for itself may be formulated as a reaction against the hegemony of the two tendencies mentioned above: the restriction of scientific enterprise to the physical sciences, and the reductionist program. With this perspective we shall now attempt to show its aims and methods.

According to the orientation of phenomenology, philosophy and science merge and complement one another when science is understood in the light of phenomenological principles. This reunion characterizes the current phase of the interrelations of philosophy and science. Phenomenological philosophy intends to provide a methodological basis for all fields of inquiry, a basis which satisfies the criteria of precision and verifiability and which is fundamental to all methods—regarding the scientific method, narrowly conceived, as a special case. Thus phenomenology restores to the term "scientific" its traditional broader meaning while recognizing the specific differences between the physical sciences, the social sciences, and the sciences of man, the last embracing psychology, psychiatry, and other fields of *Geisteswissenschaften*.

The elaboration of new methodological distinctions and techniques enables one to avoid oversimplification and fallacious reductions, e.g., the reduction of culture to economic conditions or of higher mental phenomena to the sublimation of natural drives. On phenomenological grounds new dimensions of human life are recognized as autonomous, many rejected factors of cognition are reinstated, new data are taken into account, and a new basis of cognitive evaluation is established. These developments will be explicated in this book by focusing upon three of the most significant achievements in contemporary thought: (1) Edmund Husserl's foundation of an absolutely certain knowledge, to which the two others ultimately refer, (2) the recognition of a new dimension of human life, *Existenz,* as elaborated by

Karl Jaspers and (3) Martin Heidegger's non-physicalistic conception of the world.

Husserl's phenomenological foundation for universally valid inquiry, although revolutionary, has been generally adopted in many fields. For the first time in history many inquiries are being pursued with a clear awareness of their philosophical commitments with respect to their methods and their underlying philosophical orientation.

After a discussion of Husserl's principles, interpreted as the opening of a new field of investigation, there follows a series of sections showing some of the phenomenological techniques engendered by Husserl's basic phenomenological method. An attempt is made to formulate the common structural pattern of the disparate techniques employed in phenomenologically oriented inquiries.

The sections following the discussion of Jaspers' conception of the *existential encounter* will exhibit phenomenological techniques operating within a new dimension, the relation to the other person. The creative aspect of interpersonal relations illuminates research in psychology, sociology, law, economics, etc., and generates the concept of dynamic man interacting with a social world.

Finally, after an examination of Heidegger's conception of the world, in which the pivotal concepts of space and time are understood in terms of intentional phenomena, we will attempt to illustrate the spatio-temporal nature of psychological phenomena themselves by results obtained in psychology and psychopathology.

From the consideration of these three ultimate issues in methodology, metaphysics, and "anthropology," there emerges a new perspective of man and his destiny, a perspective shown in our last section which deals with existential psychoanalysis. Our approach is intended to culminate in a comprehensive view of man and the world within a unique system of meanings which may be interpreted in terms of man's concerns, emotions, actions, and his intellectual and spiritual life. Superseding the concept of the mind alienated from physical nature we discover a homogeneous universe, an essential human reality.

*Phenomenology and Science
in Contemporary European Thought*

ONE : *Apodictic Foundation of Knowledge*

1. Husserl's phenomenology opening the field of inquiry

Ever since the dialogues of Plato a great deal of attention has been paid to determining the criteria for certain knowledge: *episteme,* as opposed to mere opinion: *doxa.* In the *Republic,* Socrates examines why mathematical cognition belongs to the realm of *episteme,* and comes to the conclusion that it does for two reasons: (1) Number and mathematical objects are obtained through adequate cognition: *noesis* or intellectual intuition. (2) Mathematical science employs strict, rigorous methods which are, moreover, related to the particular nature of mathematical objects. These two aspects of knowledge, enunciated so clearly by Plato, have been from that time on one of the deepest concerns of philosophers in general. A substantial portion of the history of philosophy has been the search for a certain, indubitable cognition, employing this or that "rigorous" method and postulating, in addition, the view that fundamental ideas (axioms) are given as *self-evident*. These two, a rigorous method and self-evident axioms, have become criteria of science. Here it is enough to mention Descartes' doctrine of universal doubt overcome finally by the overwhelming evidence of the *Cogito ergo sum* and his preoccupation with a scientific method which in the *Discourse on Method* becomes a procedure *more geometrico*. It should be noted that for Descartes, use of the geometrical method insures the rigor achieved by the mathematical sciences, and in this respect Descartes initiated modern science and philosophy. Descartes' ideal of mathematical rigor was taken over by such rationalists as Spinoza, Leibniz, Wolff, whose systems were based on the deduction of theorems from accepted self-evident principles and also attempted to assure the certainty of cognition by strict methods of procedure.

In contemporary thought this tradition has been represented by two very influential tendencies. It has been asserted that if philosophy can be confined to logical questions, then its ideal of being a rigorous science can be achieved, and this has been the intent of the symbolic logic of the present century. The clarity and precision of symbolic logic's formulation, its deductive procedure, its exactness and brevity of language seem to fulfil Descartes' dream of philosophy formulated in "clear and distinct ideas." However, as has often been pointed out, neither logic nor any deductive science can convey the ultimate cognition of the universe and man. The reason, as expressed for example by Marvin Farber,[1] is the limitation on the deductive method imposed by the problem of meaning. The deductive method operates on a high level of abstraction; so high that it cannot grasp less abstract meanings with their reference to the concrete data of experience. To use Farber's expression: "meanings lie before" it as a pre-logical sphere and in their complexity cannot be brought to the level of logical clarification and systematization. The most basic knowledge exemplified in meanings has its roots in the cognition of the world itself and the things of the world. This cognition of the world can, therefore, never reach the logical level. And this immediate cognition of the world has always been the object of philosophical inquiry. This serves to explain why the scientific ideal of mathematical rigor has not yet been achieved in philosophy. On the contrary, the deductive procedure in metaphysics has lost all credit in the last decades, being strongly rejected by philosophers like Nicolai Hartmann as merely a rationalistic speculation.

On the other hand, at the beginning of our century, empirical naturalism sought criteria for the validity of knowledge in a self-governing Reason, which it regarded as the only authority in matters of truth. In the search for an exclusively valid cognition, as opposed to various prejudices perpetuated by "tradition and superstition," naturalists adopted a methodological radicalism. In such a view to pass a rational judgment about facts means that *facts themselves* have to be questioned. In their *self-givenness* facts must guide our judgment to the exclusion of all prejudice. A return to facts is identified here with a return to experience. And so the naturalist confines the knowable facts to those that are knowable through the senses, and hence the realm of facts is limited to nature, and scientific inquiry is confined to a consideration of natural facts. In life and scholarship we deal constantly with facts of art, culture, social life and institutions. How, then, can a naturalistic, scientific view be adequate to the world as we find it in our everyday experience? It would seem that, indeed, the acceptance of facts of nature as the only ground for judgment without prior investigation is a prejudice in itself. The absolute rejection of all judgment alien to experience seems to limit severely the framework of scientific and philosophic inquiry.

There is one thing we must remember: both logical positivism and naturalistic empiricism agree upon this basic issue. Both seek fundamental knowledge about the world through the results of the empirical sciences. These "physically anchored" results can be expressed in quantitative terms, and so can approach mathematical brevity and exactness. They can be easily arranged into axiomatic systems. Yet sciences using empirical methods (like the behavioral sciences) relinquish the criterion of *indubitable* cognition; they give up the criterion of *evidence* and exchange it for the cognition that is merely *verifiable*. Judged by the new criteria, philosophy (by incorporating uncritically the scientific results into more general considerations) renounces any claim to be a rigorous science exemplifying certain knowledge: *episteme;* the classical ideal is reduced to a more general pseudo-scientific hypothesis based upon probable, verifiable statements: a technically elaborated form of *doxa*. Some pragmatists and "logical empiricists" [2] consider even the demand for cognitive certainty to be an unrealizable goal. Lacking new criteria for the validity of philosophical cognition, they dismiss the whole question together with other problems that are related to it in traditional philosophy as meaningless. From this perspective, philosophical inquiry is either compelled to provide (and this to the exclusion of everything else) a general interpretation of the particular sciences, or to resolve limited problems which emerge in the analysis of scientific and ordinary discourse.

Philosophers with such a point of view, when confronted by the challenge that science makes to philosophy, seek (along with the scientists) to establish a common ground of inquiry in the scientific inquiry itself. However, Edmund Husserl, at the beginning of this century, proposed another method of unifying the particular sciences and philosophy. Husserl's method was not in opposition to traditional ideals, and was based upon a foundation which was philosophical and apodictic. Several philosophers who followed in Husserl's footsteps have used his discoveries to penetrate the realm of philosophy itself. Results obtained from the researches of these philosophers have greatly influenced European scholarship in general.

In his attempt to make philosophy resume its role of a universal and basic science, Husserl sought to lay the foundation for philosophy as a rigorous science (*strenge Wissenschaft*). He gave a challenging answer to all three of the controversial issues: philosophy, instead of being reduced to a pseudo-scientific hypothesis, can exemplify *certain* and *indubitable* knowledge; philosophy can be a rigorous science despite non-deductive methods; and it is a specifically philosophical task to investigate the ground for valid judgments.

Husserl's philosophical principles sprang from the same motives as those of empirical naturalism. Indeed, phenomenology shares with empirical naturalism the tendency toward an intellectual radicalism, which (opposing the powers of tradition and superstition) seeks to establish self-governing reason as the sole authority in scholarship. Furthermore, the deep concern of naturalism can be interpreted as a search for an instance of cognition where objects of cognition are characterized by self-givenness. Empirical intuition, specifically perception, brings the individual object to "givenness" as Husserl says, in a "primordial" way, in what he calls its "bodily selfhood." It seems this way of appearing in "bodily presence" gives the objects of perception their privileged position among other objects, such as memory or imagination. However, Husserl shows that it is merely due to prejudice that this primordial way of givenness is considered as proper to sensory objects alone. On the contrary, inspired by Franz Brentano, Husserl establishes at the outset of his philosophical endeavor that "every possible object, or to put it logically, 'every subject of possible true predications' has . . . its *own* way . . . of coming under a glance that presents, intuits, meets it eventually in its 'bodily selfhood' and 'lays hold of it.' " [3]

Furthermore, if what we call intuition is a cognitive instance presenting an object to us as "self-given," then such intuition is more basic than a specific form of it: sensory intuition. Husserl calls intuition in this basic cognitive function an "instituting act." [4]

Through this basic and larger conception of intuition, Husserl replaces sensory experience as the only authority for cognition and ground for judgments; thereby his separation from naturalism is achieved. This acceptance means that *whatever presents itself in 'intuition' in primordial form* (as it were in its bodily reality) *is simply to be accepted as it gives itself to be, though only within the limits in which it then presents itself.*" [5] This assertion constitutes, as Husserl calls it, "the principle of all principles" in his philosophical foundation of scientific inquiry; it contains a whole program.

It remains to be seen, however, what is the nature of such a cognitive instance, one which allows *all* possible objects of judgment to present themselves in their bodily presence. As early as his *Logische Untersuchungen*[6] Husserl introduced and elaborated the notion of the *eidetic* or *essential intuition*. This was meant to be the intuition of objects grasped at the level of their essential structures. As such this basic notion implies two correlated elements: (1) a specific type of conscious act in which such intuition can be performed and a corresponding theory of consciousness, and (2) a theory of objects as possessing intrinsic, essential natures, *essences* or *eidoi*. The strict correlation between the object of cognition and the act of consciousness achieved in terms of the *intentionality* of consciousness, is the pivotal point of Husserl's foundation of phenomenology. However, the notion of eidetic intuition as an instituting act where *all* objects of true predication can be self-given (albeit in their own ways), is the cornerstone of Husserl's foundation of phenomenological inquiry in various fields.

Against the possibility of deducing certain knowledge of the concrete world from one or few principles (axioms), as for example Descartes' *cogito* or Spinoza's *substance,* Husserl opposes the affirmation that there is more than one *certain, evident,* immediately given object of cognition. According to him, the circumambient world consists of "self-evident" things; that is, objects of cognition.

To the demand for a deductive procedure, which would obtain knowledge additional to that offered by self-evident objects, Husserl asserts that such objects alone can provide us with the answers to all philosophical questions. The simple description of their features provides us with strict connections and necessary laws capable of replacing deductive rigor. The question of the certainty of their cognition is not, according to Husserl, a matter of self-evidence (whereby some categories of objects, as for example Plato's ideas, would have a priority over others), but rather involves the method by which their cognition is achieved. The employment of such a method would open up the universe to fundamental philosophy.[7]

The method elaborated by Husserl (called "phenomenological reduction" or "époché") consists of suspending successively certain of the natural, customary aspects and components of our cognition. All of these constitute preconceptions about what is to be discovered. Thus transformation of our cognitive attitude from the *natural*—providing only confused, uncertain cognition—to the "reflexive attitude" (in Husserl's view) opens the field of *apodictically* certain knowledge. The first fundamental postulate of the method is that knowledge of an object is limited to that content of cognition factually ascertainable in the corresponding act of consciousness. But what can be factually found in the perception of an object which is basic to all empirical sciences? The second basic concern of the phenomenological method is to discover what content can provide a *certain,* adequate cognition of its object.

How the critical results attained by the phenomenological method are related to empirical cognition, so that they cover the whole realm of cognition thereby endowing it with certainty, will be analyzed later.[8]

In the "natural" attitude our experiences, in all realms, emerge from our connection with the world.[9] I am aware of the world which constitutes the horizon of all my experiences. It contains everything, including men; the world constitutes my immediately given field within which I see whatever is as "being there," *existing.* Consequently, in every cognitive or evaluative act we implicitly posit an existential judgment about the world and ourselves. Furthermore, it is natural to posit the world as being a vague shape and constructed from our cognitions, accidentally and uncritically gathered from common sense experience, scientific theories, arbitrary evaluations, beliefs, etc. Thus, every cognitive act effected naturally already carries with it the predecision about what it is supposed to provide: an essential, unprejudiced cognition of the object in question. It is precisely because of these preconceptions that the Cartesian doubt arises: Do I exist, does the world exist (since our experience gives such a contradictory view of the world)? This natural attitude is rooted in empirical experience, and is based upon sensory (outer and inner) perception. And it is of the nature of this perception, as in Descartes' example of the piece of wax, to see an object as first endowed with some properties, and then with other properties taking the place of the former, according to the different circumstances in time and space where perception is achieved. However, if the given object of perception is considered apart from all aspects of the act of cognition (in its natural form)—which Husserl considers to preconceive the cognitive act itself—the same object still remains.

Husserl's analysis shows that the components of perception which prejudice us about its object are: its factual existence, the preconception that the object belongs to the natural world, the preconception that its cognition results from a psycho-physiological stimulus-response relationship, the preconceptions derived from previous uncritical assumptions, and those stemming from the whole psycho-physiological part of the perception. He also indicates that when we abstract from all these and other more refined preconceptions, the object still in the field of perception, cleared of all its changes of character relative to the empirical conditions of experience, *displays itself* in its essentially rational structure, which constitutes the object's nucleus. This rational nucleus can be identified unchanged in any adequate perception of the object in question, as its *ti esti*. The object represented by its rational structure is present, not as a natural object, but merely as a *cogitatum*.

In short: the suspension of the enumerated "naturalistic" components of perception has permitted the passage from the "natural" to the "reflexive" attitude. This latter is supposed to be free from empirical preconceptions, to the extent that the rational structure of the object alone is given. This structure, as a rational residuum of the natural object, *displays itself* in its *bodily presence,* showing its components to be organized by necessary connections. Here we must understand what Husserl calls "phenomena": objects of cognition, insofar as they immediately display themselves to consciousness. To display the essential nature—permanent features within necessary connections—of "phenomena," Husserl more specifically refers to Aristotle, calling them *"eidos"* or *"essence" (Wesen, Wesenheit).*

Emphasizing the radical difference between natural perception (empirical, sensory) and the way in which the same objects of cognition display themselves after reduction to the reflexive attitude, Husserl calls the perception of phenomena, "categorial perception" or—referring to the above-mentioned specific nature of a phenomenon—"eidetic insight," "eidetic intuition." The categorial perception is understood to be based on what is given to the senses, but at the same time to be constructed upon it.

What then is the *eidos* or *essence* with respect to empirical perception and its content? Take an example from the realm of artistic creativity. The child with a pigeon, painted by Picasso, presents properties of a child indistinguishable in natural perception from those of any child. Nevertheless the painter has reproduced something which the closest imitation of a child (perceived by the senses) would be unable to bring out, namely, childhood itself in its universality—inadequate, still present in every individual child, whatever his individual properties be—the *essence* of a child. Contemporary art is characterized by its effort toward *eidetic* perception. The most striking examples are offered by the musical, tonal transposition of what otherwise belongs to visual perception. De Falla's *Nights in the Gardens of Spain,* Debussy's *Pagode* present an *essence* of Spanish gardens or of a pagoda in musical reproduction, more pagoda-like and more typical of Spanish gardens than any visual, empirical perception of a pagoda or of a garden in Spain could be. Rainer Maria Rilke's *The Book of Images* is another example of how things and feelings can be reproduced in their universality; this makes great artists. Of course the artist needs first natural perception. He needs to see colors, hear tones, etc. This perception, however, is, for his creativity, merely a starting point to grasp the universal and a medium in which to reproduce it. If the reproduction of sensory data alone sufficed for his creativity, photography could replace painting.

In mathematics such an *eidos,* or phenomenological essence, is present in the pure mathematical concepts of a number, a straight line, a triangle, or a circle, in contradistinction to triangles, circles, and straight lines drawn on a piece of paper. However skillfully a circle can be drawn, it will never be *exactly* equivalent to what is understood by the essential concept of a circle; it will always remain an approximation. It is from the *eidetically* perceived *eidos* of a triangle or a circle, with the necessary connections of its structure, that connections are stated in mathematics as axioms and theorems. That in mathematical science we can form *a priori* statements and judgments, is due to *eidetic* insight. On the other hand, if a geometer dealing with empirically "embodied" lines, triangles, circles in iron and chalk can validate statements about them and their relations, it is because from the approximative character of their natural presentation he refers by *eidetic* insight to the *eidos* of a circle and triangle (pure Euclidean geometry).

In the same way that geometric insights "apply" to the spatial forms of nature, so do the *eidetic* insights of psychological processes and experiences correspond to the natural (empirical) experiences of animal beings. It was Husserl's conviction, which underlay his project of the phenomenological research, that there could be no factual science free from *eidetic* insights and thereby not dependent on an inquiry by the phenomenological method. Furthermore, not only things and beings, processes and events, but also all "pure objects of thought" (for example concepts, predicates, states of affairs) display their rational structure in categorial perception. Consequently the whole universe of cognition would be open to *eidetic* inquiry.

An important misconception concerning Husserl's categorial perception must be avoided. Phenomenology has often been misinterpreted as presupposing *eidos,* essence, as an ideal entity privileged by a specific ontological status, thus to represent a modern form of Platonic realism. On the contrary, the phenomenological *eidos* is conceived as being definitely beyond the epistemological controversy of idealism-realism. The phenomenological essence is by no means to be identified with Plato's *idea* as a *real* entity opposed to concrete beings, the cognition of the idea being separated from the cognition of concrete beings and opposed to empirical (natural) cognition.

To clarify this issue let us consider more precisely the relation between empirical cognition, particularly as exemplified in introspective psychological description, and phenomenological cognition, the "pure *eidetic* insight." [10] On the one hand, an abyss exists between natural and *eidetic* cognition (as far as the new import of categorial perception is concerned). But on the other hand, Husserl insists on the intimate connection between psychology and phenomenology. He emphasizes the gradual development of the phenomenological method and procedure, from empirical cognition as its origin and its source of individual facts (*Einzeltatsachen*) leading to the view of *eidetic* structures. In fact, no radical break is seen as existing in the cognitive process which leads from empirical to categorial perception. Rather in this process there is a modification, a transformation of the cognitive act without a cutting-off of its roots in empirical perception. In view of this continuity then, would phenomenology be anything other than the descriptive (introspective) psychology of Brentano or Dilthey?

According to Husserl and to psychologists who have adopted the phenomenological method, the two are not the same. The first difference would be that a descriptive psychologist, in spite of considering the object of inquiry—for example, a perceptual act—within the limits of what is factually contained in the act itself (immanent to consciousness), still considers the act in question as a *real* (natural) experience, which he can think of only as being related to a *real* (natural) human being—a part of nature. In *eidetic* or transcendental phenomenology this last preconception of nature disappears. If the natural bias of experience is suspended, the whole complex of judgments referring to the performer of conscious acts as a part of nature is also suspended, and left for a specific inquiry. What remains thereafter is a "pure phenomenological residuum": consciousness understood as source of *cogitationes.* These *cogitationes* exhibit necessary, rational connections between themselves, thus constituting the universe of an *eidetic* science.

There is a second difference between a psychological description and phenomenology. A descriptively oriented psychologist limits his attention to a consideration of singularities, individual acts or processes. A phenomenologist, on the contrary, takes these singularities only as a point of departure from which to advance gradually toward general essences. It is here that one proceeds from a singular act of "outer perception" toward the *essence* of "outer perception," to proceed from the "inner act" of "inner perception" toward the categorial perception. These two differences specify the method of phenomenological reduction.

In conclusion: the *absolute certainty* of the phenomenological method and cognition is held to consist in the immediate grasp of self-evident objects displaying their rational structures, free of all preconceptions and the contingent aspects proper to simple natural cognition. This absolute certainty, although revealed by the evidence of the mode of givenness, relies on neither its subjective appeal nor on a special theory for its validation. The phenomenological evidence comes to light only when specific methodological conditions are fulfilled: first, the phenomenological reduction eliminates presuppositions; second, it simultaneously opens the field of the permanent structures of objects. When judgment is suspended concerning the *factual,* naturalistic status of objects and all random acquired notions, then all aspects of the objects of the inquiry lie bare for an *eidetic* analysis. The *eidetic* insight which directly performs that analysis is related to the assumption made at the start of the Husserlian investigation: the assumption that objects of cognition and acts of cognition are essentially correlated and correspondent. However, in order that intentional cognitive acts, which comprehend a full record of the features of objects (natural as well as *eidetic*), may bring into focus the purely structural, *eidetic* level, the two methodological conditions mentioned are required. At this level all objects of knowledge can be examined.

Thus the phenomenological method opens the field to a universal inquiry which is founded on absolutely (apodictically) certain knowledge. The certainty of this foundation consists, first, in clearing the ground for knowledge from presuppositions; second, in elaborating the notions of cognitive media in correlation with the nature of the objects of cognition—"the principle of all principles"; third, in adducing the specific type of cognitive insight and evidence thus prepared. Having ascertained that all objects of cognition can be objects of categorial perception, and having recognized that no science, whether deductive or reductive (empirical), would be free from *eidetic* insights, Husserl sees the task of phenomenology as that of clarifying fundamental ideas with the aim of unifying all the sciences at the level of their permanent and absolutely certain foundations.

2. Phenomenological techniques

The phenomenological approach is almost universally accepted by European philosophers.[11] Moreover, fulfilling Husserl's expectations, the significance of the basic achievements of phenomenology extends far beyond the limits of philosophy to the particular sciences, and important work has been done not only in the humanistic sciences such as history and theory of art but also in such empirical sciences as anthropology and economics.[12] However, the great diversity of philosophical doctrines which seem to have nothing in common except their professed allegiance to phenomenological method raises the question as to whether this diversity has more than a nominal unity. A brief consideration of methodology is offered now to clarify this crucial question.

Husserl's phenomenology has provided a basis for inquiry by opening a field, clearing it of methodological and other presuppositions, and indicating the locus of a new method. The method has been characterized in general as analytic, with the objective of delineating the permanent structures of objects. However, the technical aspects of phenomenological analysis have been left vague and unsystematic. For analytic methods to be workable when applied to specific subject matters, appropriate techniques are required which will be capable of organizing inquiries into special fields. These techniques must be able to deal with the specific nature of those particular subject matters, and must also provide frameworks for the categorization of the results obtained.

The specific objective which Husserl proposed for phenomenological analysis presupposes that a given subject matter will be revealed as structured in a certain way, and that areas of research can be classified and distinguished on the basis of the different types of structures exhibited. Therefore phenomenological techniques should be able to deal with structural organizations. But the methodological justification of these techniques would require the discovery of universal structural laws.

When Husserl's eidetic analysis was applied to specific subject matters by post-Husserlian thinkers, the highly technical potentialities of the analysis came to light. It is our contention that the phenomenological method particularizes itself into several techniques of inquiry, thereby developing commitments to various subject matters. But, if this is so we must ask ourselves, How can the multiplicity of separate techniques be claimed to be instances of a phenomenological method? Can the different commitments to the various subject matters account for the doctrinal diversity in the phenomenological current?

At first glance it would seem that this welter of "methods" has little in common with the rigorous analysis practiced by Husserl. The various techniques appear to be only fragments of that vast structural analysis Husserl conceived. What is more, it is often difficult to trace their historical connections with Husserl's principles, and it is nearly impossible to establish the extent to which those principles were explicitly adopted and to what extent they are in accord with phenomenological intentions. That some reference is made to phenomenology does not of course mean that the term is not used arbitrarily. Thus the crucial question is whether one can determine the extent to which the analytic techniques draw upon phenomenology, what this common ground is, and what is the relationship of the results obtained.

It is our contention that it is only through a methodological investigation that such a common ground can be discovered. Our view will, I think, be borne out by examination of a *structural model* [13] which incorporates and corroborates Husserl's initial principles while guaranteeing the final co-ordination of otherwise disparate results.

In our introduction we pointed out how Continental thought at the close of the nineteenth century and the beginning of the twentieth was dominated by the reductive tendencies of the evolutionary, historical, relativistic approach. Dependent upon Darwin's theory of biologic evolution, Spencer's extension of it to social phenomena, and Hegel's historical development of spirit, the sciences and humanities attempted to explain their complex data by reducing them to their supposed primitive origins. The origins in most cases were supposed to be of biologic nature, which meant that all intellectual, social, cultural, and spiritual phenomena would ultimately be reducible to some primitive data from which they arose through some psychological, social, historical, or biologic process. The manner in which Husserl's thought initiated a metamorphosis in this attitude has already been outlined. Phenomenology, by concentrating solely on the direct analysis of the structure of phenomena, has superseded the construction of explanatory hypotheses and revealed far more complexities in many fields than the older methods had admitted. This is doubtless the most significant *general* accomplishment of phenomenology and will be a recurrent theme in the remainder of this essay. The phenomenological approach appears self-explanatory; consequently, the evidence from direct insight obviates the hypothetico-causal approach.

However, it has been generally ignored how *special* models and techniques of investigation in various fields were scrutinized and revolutionized by phenomenology. The most prominent procedures of the new phenomenological techniques are: (1) differentiating fields of inquiry by their specific nature, followed by analyses limited to aspects appropriate to the particular objectives; (2) establishing "models" of inquiry consisting of multilayered structures; and (3) determining irreducible elements, qualities, patterns, or norms. But what guarantee is there that these fragments of inquiry have a common ground in phenomenology?

A methodological point of reference for deciding this question is provided by the universal phenomenological concept of structure as such. The *model of the many-layered structure* discussed in the first of the following sections is to be construed as such a reference point, and therefore requires special attention.

This model is itself the universal pattern of structure. Many "layers" can be distinguished in it, and their irreducible autonomy can be established, as well as ways of articulating their interplay. The model exhibits the specific principles used separately in structural analysis and, as a common structural pattern, still serves to co-ordinate them. However, how can the many-layered structure display the principles of structural analysis? The answer is that it constitutes the key to the structural unity of any entity or object of cognition which is thought to be a complex of heterogeneous elements (as, for example, the sound of a word and its intellectual meaning). The many-layered organization emphasizes the heterogeneity of elements, but at the same time organizes them into an organic unity by means of the hierarchical stratification and interlayer connections. The specific uniqueness of each component is preserved and, through the general pattern of organization, they are established as autonomous in terms of layers; in addition this structural mechanism and its modes of operation point out several types of possible connections. Through the appropriate application of these connections, autonomous layers become incorporated into an organic whole.

Consequently, in the structural analysis referring to the universal model of many-layered structure, the complexity of the subject matter must be accepted at the outset of any inquiry, and the inquiry regarded as the search for specific components intrinsic to the subject matter as its irreducible residua. An initial allowance of a flexible set of categories should be adopted to facilitate the grasping of specific heterogeneous elements, and an initial allowance of more than one type of interlayer connections should make possible the recognition of various sorts of structural mechanisms. This last methodological postulate is crucial to the phenomenological orientation, for if causal relations are the only sort admitted, as in the reductionistic approach, then every object is capable of being reduced to its causal relations, its "reasons." However, the autonomy of various realms of being presupposes relations other than causal.

In this way the model of many-layered structure shows how various phenomenological techniques can be co-ordinate and yet compatible with a disparity of specific doctrines arising from their disparate results.

In the sections which follow, after an extensive presentation of the model of many-layered structure, we will show how the search for irreducible residua takes the form of "intrinsic" analysis in the study of literature, aesthetics, art, and culture. The autonomy of different fields of inquiry will be shown to suggest further techniques in psychology and psychopathology: delimitation of distinctive domains of research and of methods appropriate to the specific subject matters; specific methods of dealing with mental phenomena; the acceptance of "motivation" as a noncausal but efficacious kind of connection. In the study of intelligence conceived in behavorial terms the many-layered model appears as a prototype of a structural mechanism integrating apparently irreconcilable levels of human functioning, ranging from the sensory-motor functions of biological adaptation to the highest intellectual activities. In anthropology we shall see three basic methods—experimental (empirical), structural, and mathematical—incorporated into one process of investigation.

It may well be that the supreme methodological achievement of the many-layered model is that it outlines a pattern of all-inclusive investigation, in which all properly scientific methods—for centuries practiced within mutually exclusive and narrow boundaries—may at last co-operate.[14]

1. *The model of a stratified structure*

Nicolai Hartmann has emphasized the far-reaching significance of the strata-approach. He directly relates the discovery of the many-layered structure and the extent to which it has been adopted in contemporary thought to one universal concern, the desire to restore the inquiries concerning man to their full dimensions, thus doing justice to man's complete nature.[15] To Max Scheler must go the credit for being a pioneer in the field. By distinguishing various layers or strata of emotional life he created a new approach to the treatment of psychological problems.[16] However, the theoretical clarification and foundation of the strata-approach had to wait until the analysis of the literary work of art by Roman Ingarden.[17]

The structure of the literary work of art seems particularly significant for the strata-approach since it incorporates three strata intrinsic to the world, strata whose autonomy is a recurrent issue in all reductionistic controversies concerning man: the physical, the intelligible, and the spiritual.

Ingarden's detailed analysis of the literary work of art runs parallel to the attempts of the New Critics and to the foundation of the contemporary "objective" or "intrinsic" trend in art criticism. It can also be directly applied to the study of culture and the history of ideas.

The specific problems on which Ingarden concentrates are: (1) What is the nature and mode of being of an entity presented in an aesthetic experience? (2) What is the mode of being of an entity confronting us when we read or hear a word, phrase, or sentence? and (3) how is this entity related simultaneously to both consciousness and independent realities?

Provisionally restricting the discussion to the second problem, the crucial issue is this: "How is intersubjective identity, and thus communication, possible?" [18] The answer to this question involves not only the possibilities of history, science, and philosophy, but implicates also the nonlinguistic media of communication. And so the issue becomes the question of whether or not all media of communication have a common intelligible or intuitive content which makes possible human institutions, social life, and culture.

Ingarden has pointed out that the task in the appreciation and understanding of art is to perceive and analyze the nature of the entity which in itself is the work of art. In this Ingarden opposed the then dominant criteria for the understanding of a work of art which were in terms of the psychology or social experiences of—or the historical influences upon—the creative artist, making the intrinsic content of a work of art relative to individual or social psychology and a product of a historical process. Thus, as P. Leon emphasized in his review which introduced Ingarden's work to the English-speaking public in 1931, "he [Ingarden] makes a resolute and much-needed attempt to save this discipline (literary criticism, aesthetics) from being nothing but a tittle-tattle of psychology." [19] To this end Ingarden established "objective" norms as a standard of the aesthetic value of a work of art. Instead of reducing the extreme complexity of a work of art to some hypothetically primitive factors—for example, to the psychology of the creative experience—Ingarden has shown that a work of art, upon appropriate examination, will explicitly reveal its own inherent structure without need of any explanatory theory. Accordingly, two original and most important points can be distinguished as a consequence of the revelation of the structure of a work of art. In the first place, a distinction can be made between the work of art and its many *concretions*. Secondly, the composition of a work of art can be seen to consist of several specific *strata,* or *layers,* of a heterogeneous nature. The culminating point of the inquiry consists in establishing the homogeneous unity of the work of art in spite of the fact that each of the several specific strata composing it possesses its own nature and its own different mode of being. The progressive analysis of the work of art leads to the revelation of how such disparate strata can together constitute the organic unity of an aesthetic object.

Specifically, Ingarden establishes four strata evident in the literary work of art which are integrated in a certain order following the different existential realms to which they individually belong.[20]

The first stratum of the literary work is that of sound. Sounds, in general, are of the real, existing world and possess, essentially, two aspects: first of all, we distinguish between the sound units of individual words and of higher sound formations (sentences and sentence concatenation); secondly, for their concretion, they must be vocalized, which endows them with properties of their own (for example, sonority, rhythm, and tempo).[21] Even at this level, however, an important observation must be made: the particular utterances do not make the work of art. The individual, material sounds—their modulations being a product of the individual's utterance and circumstances—support only the concretions of the work. The literary work of art itself at this level on the contrary, consists of a constant, typical sound structure, concretized "the same" in all individual utterances of a text; however, the sound structure needs these modulations in order to be concretized, as for example when a poem is read or a play performed. This constant sound structure is responsible for the identity of the work of art, in spite of the infinite variations of its performance in perception. The individual material sounds and sound formations of a novel, poem, or drama remain "the same" in spite of the fact that they differ in tone, pitch, accent, modulation, and so on, not only, for example, each time the rôle of Hamlet is played by a different actor, but also with each performance. The major problem now becomes evident. Although borne by the physical sound material, this persistent structure of sounds and their formations cannot exist or be real because it could not then be present and the same in different sound occurrences. The sound structure cannot be ideal (in the sense of unchangeable mathematical objects), for it comes into being as the product of a creative process, is bound to the physical sounds and changes, although, as long as a given sound structure is part of a particular context, it persists in being identical in its concretions. The problem becomes of even greater interest if we realize that sound can convey identical meanings because of the identical natures of specific sound formations. This proposition becomes the subject of inquiry of Ingarden's second stratum.

The essence of the second stratum is that the absolute sound formation cannot be reduced to component sounds because it consists of irreducible *nova*. On the other hand, the properties of the sound structures (such as sonorousness, rhythm, tempo, and so forth) exhibit aesthetic values—are *aesthetically valuable*—in terms of which the work of art or aesthetic object is constituted.

From identical sound formations emerge concatenations of *meanings* which constitute the second irreducible stratum of the literary work of art. In spite of the fact that the concatenations of meanings emerge from identical sound structures, they present a most original character. The meanings of individual words, sentences, and sentence concatenations within, for example, a narrative discourse, sketch an entity, thing, person, state of mind, feeling, and so on—objects which appear either in a static or dynamic form while unfolding their multiple qualities in a process. This "unfolding" of objects in specific circumstances (events, developments, and so on) arising from sentences and their concatenations develops into an organic, meaningful unity. All such unfolded situations together form a world of persons, things, and events belonging to a particular work of art as *its* world.

In addition, meanings have properties of their own: they can be obscure or clear, light or heavy, simple or complex, literal or symbolic and so on.

First of all, taken individually, they present a situation in a gay or somber manner, creating the climate of the moods in which the situation is exhibited; secondly, in their interplay they not only contribute to the quality of the mood but also create the style. As Ingarden says, "they are aesthetically valuable elements," forming larger aesthetically functioning complexes.[22]

From this it is obvious to what extent Ingarden's analysis can be regarded as the basis for the study of style in art and life.

Concurrently, meanings in themselves, however, have their own mode of being. Indeed, Ingarden offers a new theory of meaning, refuting the conception by which Husserl laid the foundation for objective inquiry. A meaning intentionally "signifies" (symbolizes) an object, determining it materially and formally. This significance is rooted in the physical word, but it is not the property of the word. It is, in a way, "lent to it" by the signifying act of consciousness; thus, it is not a physical entity. Neither is it identical with the individual act of consciousness; thus, the meaning is not psychical. Although it is brought about and sustained by an act of consciousness, it is *transcendent* to the act. It does not vanish with the disappearance of the particular conscious act. The same meaning can be repeatedly concretized in new conscious acts. In spite of the alteration a meaning can undergo it does not make a substantial part of our psychological acts or of the stream of experience (in the sense of William James). For example, through the repetition of a meaning in various acts, or by the direct influence of one act upon another, the meaning undergoes some alterations. This does not mean, however, that the meaning is a substantial part of each act. We can transfer the meaning to other people, "separating" it from the acts, whereas we cannot separate acts themselves from our individual experience.[23]

Therefore, meanings are not existing entities; nor are they unchangeable, ideal *speciei,* in opposition to Husserl's contention, because as Ingarden shows, they undergo modifications in subjective activities. Furthermore, were they ideal, timeless, or indestructible, all works of art, stories, lyrics, comedies, and so on, in all the variations in which they have or could be conceived or reproduced, would exist forever; thus, the artist would not be a creator but a discoverer. Meanings are, however, created and can be modified by the conscious act of the one who conceives them, intentionally "lending" identical content to them, while in the concretions the performer or spectator incorporates them into his actual experience. Ingarden's new conception of the intentional mode of being of meaningful concatenations presents it as a factor of mediation among various individual experiences. But above all, it mediates between the physical and psychical as a specific content simultaneously rooted in both, and yet autonomous and transcendent with respect to both. Only because it is simul-

taneously created by experience, yet irreducible to it—
modifiable by experience and yet separable in its own
right with respect to experience—can it mediate not only
between various acts of consciousness (for example, as a
condition of memory), but also serve as a foundation for
intersubjective communication.

From the stratum of meanings with their organic systems
emerge the *objects represented* (such as things, persons, feelings) in their specific circumstances (states of affairs, *Sach-
verhalte*). These objects, consequently, emerge as intentional beings (in opposition to Husserl's conception that
the work of art has an ideal existence); they constitute the
third irreducible stratum. The objects come into existence,
together with their qualifications, by a conscious act, and
maintain subsistence in virtue of the act, which can just as
well modify or annihilate them. However, they are not reducible to the psychical nature of the act; their modifications do not coincide with the modifications of the act.

As is commonly known, the represented objects often refer to, or resemble, the real, existing, autonomous objects of
the real world up to a certain point of necessary recogniza-
bility. It is from this resemblance that a work of art at least
partially makes its emotional appeal to the reader or spectator, who assimilates its fictitious content and experiences the
objects and events represented "as if they were real." The
historical and the social approaches emphasize this resemblance with regard to the work of art and then try to reduce
its significance to a matter of historical evolution or to a matter of the social habits of human institutions. Ingarden's
conception of intentional, meaningful structure, on the
other hand, opens up new avenues of inquiry into the relation between the objects represented and their real correlates.

In fact, the stratum of objects unfolding in their specific
circumstances does not make them as fully determined as,

for example, their real, existing correlates. The real, existing Othello had a complete set of fundamental human properties, including all such individual features as a specific size of shoe, color of eyes, and so on. Thus, death, as a concrete event, has a complete set of circumstantial features among which none of its causes or manifestations is lacking. In a work of art, however, we face objects not fully determined, but displayed only from some significant point of view. Objects in a work of art are presented in chosen schematic patterns in clear-cut situations or developments which, as Aristotle would say, imitate nature "for better or worse." These shapes, views or appearances, perspectives, and clear-cut situations or developments, in which the presented objects appear constitute the fourth stratum emerging from the third as an irreducible *novum*.

The space and time perspectives in which objects are represented—distances between represented events, and so on, as well as the schematic viewpoints and other means by which a character becomes revealed—have particularly important aesthetic functions. Through their choice they produce the style of the characters, events, and atmosphere; and they also play a purely decorative rôle.[24]

This most original insight into the nature of the work of art enables us to see more clearly the specific, intentional nature of the work of art as such. In the work of art itself objects are given only schematically, fragmentarily, in perspectives purposely chosen by the artist. It is up to the individual, subjective experience of the reader or spectator, creator or performer, to make them complete in the form of a concretion. This need for turning the sketch into a complete form in the concrete with the help of individual experience is nothing other than its "intentionality." It explains how the various concretions of the same work of art can be interpreted, appreciated, and evaluated disparately by different spectators, while at the same time the work of art offers an undisputably identical nucleus of intersubjective elements and values which permits people to recognize it as "the same" work of art. Also, it enables one to establish its inherent, historically accepted value.

Each of the four strata previously mentioned, if taken separately, merely exists for itself, but they are all most intimately interwoven in the work of art to form an "organic unity." However, their intimate interplay would not result in a work of art but in a mere construction if they did not also function as aesthetic values. A work of art, considered in its aesthetic sense, displays a specific, intangible glamor, resulting from the merging of the constitutive elements. The work of art as an aesthetic object is the precise consequence of a "polyphonic harmony" of the aesthetically valuable qualities.[25] Although the recognition of the purely aesthetic significance of a work of art is contingent to some extent upon subjective, individual differences in appreciation, the recognition finds an "objective" foundation because it emerges from the objective realms of the strata mentioned. In this light, the most confusing and the most "esoteric" questions—for example, questions of meaning and value of a work of art—find an unequivocal, objective foundation.

As a matter of fact, the apex of aesthetic value in the work, emerging as a product of the previously mentioned aesthetically valuable elements and in particular from the objects represented, is the specific atmosphere wherein the represented events, persons, and circumstances move, together with their specific aspects. This atmosphere has an over-all representative quality (or qualities): of the sublime, tragic, terrible, demoniacal, sinful, holy, of the "undescribable brightness of happiness," the comic, ugly, and so on. These qualities are not properties of objects, events represented, or psychical acts concretizing them. On the contrary, this outburst of *metaphysical qualities* is rooted mainly in the stratum of the objects represented; but they participate in the aesthetically valuable qualities, such as sonorousness, style, and so on, of all the remaining strata. On the other hand, it is in the manner in which these metaphysical qualities come to be revealed that the most genuine artistic achievement lies. This revelation is built up and often announced by various phases in which it momentarily glimmers, before its point of culmination is reached. In order that this revelation may come about, all strata ought to co-operate in harmony.

The metaphysical qualities play a salient aesthetic rôle in the work of art. "The polyphonic harmony," Ingarden says in summary, "is precisely that 'aspect' of the literary work of art which, together with the metaphysical qualities (which come to be revealed in a work of art), makes the work a *work of Art*." [26]

Although the revelation of every specific object in terms of values tends to make it appear as a work of Art, Ingarden insists on the insufficiency of this construction of objects considered alone, saying "it is only this [aesthetically valuable formation] that makes the literary work a *work of Art* (provided that, in a given work, the revelation of metaphysical qualities comes about), but it is most intimately interwoven with all other constitutive elements of the work of art." [27]

The two most significant results of Ingarden's inquiry should be stressed. First, one of the outstanding features of his analysis consists in demonstrating that several heterogeneous strata, which in the history of thought have been considered as belonging to irreconcilable realms—extending from the physical, psychical, and through the meaningful up to the metaphysical qualities of the spiritual—can enter not only into a composition but can even constitute the organic unity of a homogenous object. This insight made possible the shift in emphasis from the attempt to abolish their differences to the search for their unifying structure and their individual rôle in it.

In fact, in the realm of strictly philosophical problems, Ingarden's analysis of the interrelations between various strata within the same work of art establishes a new solution to the controversial issue hitherto formulated in terms of an irreconcilable heterogeneity between the meaningful (in particular the spiritual) and the physical. As Nicolai Hartmann formulates it, this theory reveals ". . . how a spiritual content can be fixed in a material ground.[28] And so, in technical terms, Ingarden establishes that the meaningful (together with its spiritual aspect), although emerging from the physical, the real, nevertheless undeniably exhibits its own irreducible nature with respect to its "bearer." In this manner, Ingarden refutes the legitimacy of all recurrent attempts to explain the relationship between the physical and the meaningful (especially the nature of the spiritual) by a reduction of the meaningful (or spiritual) to the physical as if "produced from" the latter by a process of evolution. On the contrary, Ingarden's inquiry exhibits the patterns of a foundation of the one in the other, thus leading to an explanation involving an exceedingly ramified mutual motivation without, however, denying their specific, irreducible natures.

As a second major contribution of this inquiry, we can consider the manner in which Ingarden conceives the unified form of the various heterogenous strata. It is the intentional nature of this homogeneous unity that permits these strata to coexist in reciprocal interplay without any of them losing their individuality. The intentional mode of being of the work of art effectuates this homogeneous unity of the strata. In other words, this unity is the result of the distinctive "objectifying" functions of the intentional act which "lends" to its objects a content separable from it.

2. *The intrinsic study of literature; norms and residua of art and culture*

a. Until the thirties literature and art in general were in a precarious position. Although expressed in public media, the content exhibited ephemeral features claimed to refer on the one hand to the creative processes of the artist, and on the other to the psychological receptivity of the percipient. Understanding the "meaning" of a work of art was reduced to explaining the work solely with reference to the biography of the artist and the psychological responses of the percipient; eventually with reference to social phenomena.

This travesty of criticism and aesthetics was challenged by Richards and the New Critics. The phenomenological strata-theory seems to have provided a theoretical basis for the new trend in literary study thus inaugurated. Emphasizing the "objective," bias-independent content of the literary work, an attempt was made to develop an objective technique of literary study. Intersubjective validity is attained by concentrating on the "intrinsic" features of the content of the work, and evaluating its worth according to norms inferred from the intrinsic nature of the work.

In their recent *Theory of Literature,* René Wellek and Austin Warren, distinguished proponents of the "objective" trend, trace their fundamentally "intrinsic" approach to the analysis of the literary work of art back to the distinctive nature and intentional existence of the literary work.[29] They detect the constituents of the literary work (euphony, rhyme, meter, style, and so on) with respect to the distinction of the basic strata and their reciprocal motivation. Conceived with reference to the "intrinsic" constituents of the work, euphony, meter, and so on, are able to constitute the norms, so long vainly looked for, to be used in the study of literature. As such, they can also be used as a basis for distinguishing literary genres.[30] Because of their treatment of the subject with detailed examples extending in an original way over the history of literature, they have been able to incorporate the strata theory into a central thesis from which it can govern the study of literary theory and history.[31]

b. Aesthetics as a general investigation into the conditions of Art and its meaning naturally vacillates between different types of relativism as long as the question of the nature of the work of art and the question of its "objective" status remains undetermined. In his recent phenomenological analysis of the nature of the aesthetic object Mikel Dufrenne works within the full climate of the general and specific acquisitions resulting from the strata-theory.[32] He takes as completely established the conception of the work of art as an intrinsically determined result of the concatenations of aesthetic values emerging from the physical, psychical, and meaningful constituents as bearers of the aesthetic content. In vivifying fashion, he illustrates the emergence of the *purely aesthetic object* from its constituents by means of numerous judiciously chosen examples. He proceeds within the context of the distinction between the work of art itself and its many concretions. On the structural basis the aesthetic object is disclosed as an objectively established, specifically aesthetic and irreducible phenomenon. Thereby the specifically aesthetic essence of art, art experience, aesthetic feeling, etc., has found a specific status and an intersubjective meaning.

c. Parallel to the tendency to explain away the aesthetic phenomenon by reducing it to psychological processes runs the tendency to understand cultural phenomena in general, with reference to their historical evolution. But, reduced to its causes, the nature of an era, an intellectual trend, or a religious spirit distintegrates or becomes grossly distorted. Only by discovering the unique residua in cultural manifestations are they truly understood.

André Malraux's guiding ideas, in his psychology of art, fall into the pattern under discussion.[33] Malraux, recognizing the specific structure of culture, abandons the conception that the origin and development of the successive stages of a culture can be understood in terms of and as an outcome of previous stages. In place of this he offers an analysis of the irreducible nature of each. In his famous *The Voices of Silence*, he brings this specific nature into sharp focus in terms of irreducible qualitative residua of cultural and especially aesthetic qualities. His main effort is to show the incommensurable perspectives for art perception and understanding by means of the subtle directions offered by the contemporary techniques of reproduction (photography, lithography, and so on) and of presentation (in organized public museums, permanent and temporary exhibitions, etc.). While accomplishing this task, the aesthetic qualities of art, of a work of art itself, emerge from Malraux's many-sided analysis as an intact, virgin identity. That is, they appear purified of all contingent constraints of the imitative, decorative, historical, and social order. The conditions of the perception and appreciation of art, insofar as they are related to certain social habits of an epoch, appear only as harmful limitations to the perception of the intangible and unique nature of the work of art thus unveiled.

3. *"Objectified Spirit" as foundation for study of ideas and culture*

Nicolai Hartmann was one of the first to adopt Scheler's distinction of layers; furthermore, he must have been acquainted with Ingarden's principles of the literary work of art and his doctrine of the "objectified" nature of various forms of the intelligible content of our feelings, utterances, and volitions in art, science, and life. He has taken it up as a leitmotif for a highly comprehensive inquiry into what we might call the foundations, life, and history of ideas.[34] He recognizes the distinction between the irreducible strata in the literary work of art and the intentionally intersubjective nature of the emerging unity, and extends the pattern of the argument by analogy, first, to all fine arts, and secondly, to the analysis of the universe and particularly to the human aspect of it.[35]

According to the pattern of strata in the universe in terms of hierarchically arranged categories (starting with the "lowest" material categories and ending with the "highest" categories, which he calls the "objectified spirit"), Hartmann distinguishes three meaningful strata with respect to the origin and life of ideas. The first stratum he recognizes is that of the individual or "personal spirit"; the second is the "objective"; and the third is the "objectified spirit." By the personal spirit is meant the complete individual psyche: volitional, conscious, and introspective. It is the personal spirit that creates and "embodies" intuitions, experiences, and values within each individual's context of life. It is man's production of such intuitions, experiences and values which makes him specifically human. Hartmann makes a distinction between spirit and consciousness. By individual consciousness he means the creative factor which also maintains a given content within an individual's consciousness. What Hartmann means by "consciousness" is, in Ingarden's terms, merely the conscious acts. By "spirit" Hartmann means what Ingarden calls the "content of an act" which, emerging from the act, takes on a distinct meaning. This meaning is separable from the act; because of this the content is separable from its ties to the individual consciousness. This separability Hartmann calls the "expansive character of the spirit." Hartmann gives an interesting treatment of the way in which the "expansive character" is related to the lower material stratum: the living organism.

Furthermore, where Ingarden merely points out, Hartmann elaborates upon the way in which the separable, intelligible content becomes incorporated into complex organic unities which develop a life of their own. By such unities he means trends of thought, various cultures (such as the spirit of ancient Greece and Rome), literary schools, religious sects, political ideologies, and so on. They not only have their distinct reality and life—that is they come into existence and die—but also have a regulative power upon individuals, forming human personalities by the individual's "participating in them" (so as to form, for example, a man of the Renaissance, a Marxist, or an "existentialist"). Their reality consists in an "intersubjective intentionality," an idea established by Ingarden, whereas in Hartmann's terms they are neither a "substance," as Hegel wrongly supposed, nor are they reducible to the individual psyche. Hartmann believes that Hegel was the first to see the independent status of the intelligible content of conscious acts but emphasizes that he misinterpreted it. Hartmann shows in detail that these contents cannot be understood in terms of excerpts and surrogates of personal experiences, but constitute, as Ingarden states, an "organic" texture of their own. However, without these contents the individual consciousness would be empty.

The "objectified spirit," as exemplified in works of art and other kinds of human creativity, denotes the meaningful content insofar as it is separable even from a living tradition. The objective spirit is, in Hartmann's terms, the hypostasis of Ingarden's intentional character of the work of art. As a matter of fact, the intersubjective contents of works of art, scientific theories, styles of art and life, of social life, ideologies, and so on, of which we have records—and which can remain meaningful to us, provided we still possess the key for deciphering them, even though the living tradition has already lost its vitality or died out—are exemplifications of the objectified spirit. Although the lowest material or psychical strata are "the strongest," Hartmann attempts to show that the "highest" strata possess a peculiar "freedom." Once they emerge, they develop in their own way.

Hartmann's intensive study further established in concrete, illustrative terms that reality will not permit itself to be treated in an oversimplified, monistic view. In less technical terms this study converts the specific insights of the strata-theory to research in the history of ideas, culture, civilization. Both Hegel and Marx were wrong in their interpretation of culture. Hegel interpreted from the top downward, in terms of "supernatural conscious substance"; Marx interpreted culture from below upward, in terms of a dialectical evolution of matter. Instead, human reality presents a far more complex situation, integrating various layers of nature and mind into an over-all structure. Consequently, Hartmann is led to a novel conception of categories and their number.[36]

4. Stratified structure applied to the psychology of intelligence

The premise that man can be adequately understood in terms of his physical functions underlies the widely used behavioral approach to psychology. In the extreme form of this view man is identified with his physical behavior, and the independent status of mental activities is denied. But the application of the techniques of structural analysis shows that this sort of account is a disastrous oversimplification. The structurally conceived organization of the entire range of human functions in terms of a functional mechanism of layers shows how wide is the diversification of functions and how distinctive and autonomous are the respective layers.

So, following the modern trend in psychology, which basically understands intelligence as a way of behavior, Jean Piaget, the Swiss psychologist, differentiates the emotive, volitional and cognitive aspects of action from each other.[37] Nevertheless, as a consequence of his approach to the analysis of behavior in terms of a stratified structure, the mythical conception of intelligence as a special mental power is destroyed. In the first place, Piaget distinguishes between the sensory-motor mechanism structures of biological adaptation and the many other structural strata of emotive and cognitive adaptation, including levels of the most complicated mental activities. Actually, the elementary sensory-motor structures of biological adaptation are stiff and one-sided. However, analysis shows that the more flexible, complex, and complete the ways of linking the acting subject with the object of his activity, the more intelligent we consider the behavior.[38] For example, perception follows a quite simple process even if its object is at some distance from the perceiver. "Intelligent" understanding, on the contrary, consisting, for example, of finding a hidden thing, or understanding a picture, presupposes multiple processes in space and time which can simultaneously be dissociated from each other and combined into other patterns. If we consider, on the one hand, the graduated complexity of various patterns or, on the other hand, their graduated flexibility (in terms of dissociation and capacity for the most complex associations), we see that these patterns must be considered in their own right. In other words, although there is a linear development of patterns from biological to complex mental activities in which each level is progressively rooted in the preceding one, the higher are nevertheless irreducible to the lower. Thus through the many-layered approach Piaget refutes the current view that the "higher" mental adaptations are reducible to the "lower" physical ones. And the too prompt equating of man and animal has been prevented. But more significant even than this are Piaget's conclusions concerning the nature of intelligence itself.

Actually, each of the specific structures of behavior remains in a more or less stable equilibrium within the narrow frame of its own realm, although each loses its stability outside its realm. Intelligence is not a particular structure of behavior but a form of equilibrium toward which all structures strive. In other words, intelligence *is* a more universal pattern which integrates all of the various structures into a higher form of organization and equilibrium.

5. *Behavior and the complexity of human nature*

Thus Piaget has disclosed the possibility of analyzing the complete gamut of man's functions within one structural pattern. In this pattern such apparently disparate functions as physiological sensory-motor activity and the highest mental activities of rational behavior are integrated and the autonomy of each preserved. The nature of the specifically human is discovered through analysis. There remains, however, the question of whether the basic levels of human behavior can be unified so as to exhibit them without distortion in a general pattern.

This has been done by Maurice Merleau-Ponty, who sees human behavior as comprised of three distinct structural layers:[39] the physical, the vital (psychophysiological), and the symbolic (meaningful). The originality of Merleau-Ponty's inquiry consists in having established that none of the three strata can be reduced to the others. The three strata are differentiated according to the traditionally established criteria of "quantity," "order," and "meaning." However, in opposition to the current view, each stratum possesses elements of the others, but in different proportions.

These differences of proportion assure the disparity of the various strata. So quantity is predominant in the physical stratum, order in the vital, and meaning in the symbolic or mental which is, of course, the most specifically human stratum.

Although irreducible to the preceding strata (contrary to Darwin's theory, man cannot be considered simply as a more highly developed animal), the symbolic stratum could not exist if it did not emerge from the integrated whole of the physical and the vital (thus man's "incarnation" is not a regrettable, accidental condition, but is "essential"). The integration of the various strata creates by a kind of dialectic one common structure—a "meaningful" body and "vitalized" mind—and through this process an integral unity with the world is also attained. The world itself in this view is no longer considered as a purely physical substance but is regarded as emerging within the same framework as man and as already a meaningful structure.

In terms of these distinctions Merleau-Ponty is confident that he has established that man has neither "exterior" nor "interior" but is all-pervaded by the meaningful as well as by the vital. Thus the long-held dichotomy between the physical and the mental vanishes.

6. *The structures of kinship in anthropology*

Claude Lévi-Strauss, in his voluminous study, based upon empirical material, opposes the hitherto prevalent evolutionary approach to anthropology through his recognition that no factual inquiry can grasp the transition from *natural* to *cultural* facts. The latter, according to him, are autonomous, "culture" being an irreducible structure—that is, one which cannot be "deduced" from more primitive elements but only described.

In his work *Les structures élémentaires de la parenté* Lévi-Strauss deals with one of the central problems in the analysis of primitive societies, namely, the kinship systems.[40] The principal feature of elementary kinship systems is that they divide the members of a society into possible and forbidden spouses according to the type of marriage from which they themselves were the issue. In every society there are certain relationships which make marriage impossible, even though the scope of the prohibition varies greatly. Lévi-Strauss is thus led to a new analysis of the problem of incest. He rejects various theories which explain the prohibition of incest on eugenic, psychological or social grounds. Rather, he characterizes the prohibition of incest as the fundamental rule which marks the difference between nature and culture. He points out that anthropoid apes apparently are completely indiscriminate in their relations, even though they tend to form more or less permanent families, whereas in every human society some limitations on marriage are enforced.

Although Lévi-Strauss therefore regards rules against incest, with the consequent formation of kinship systems, as *sui generis* to some extent, he does relate this phenomenon to the principle of reciprocity which anthropologists have observed in primitive societies. According to this principle no one can keep his concerns entirely to himself; he must share them with other members of the community. Primitive societies, therefore, present elaborate systems of gifts and barter. Contrary to the conclusions of previous anthropologists Lévi-Strauss maintains that the value of reciprocity does not lie in the commodities obtained but in that the exchange is an end in itself. It may be noted that in this respect the author returns to a much earlier idea, that of Adam Smith, who in his *Inquiry into the Nature and Causes of the Wealth of Nations,* saw man driven by a propensity to exchange goods. In the same way that primitive man regards food as a communal rather than a personal concern, he also regards women, the principal asset, as something to be exchanged with others, hence the exchange of sisters that is found in many parts of the world.

On the basis of examples drawn principally from Australia, China, India, and the American Indians, Lévi-Strauss then considers that there is only a limited number of elementary kinship systems in which a prescribed division into possible and forbidden marriage partners can be perpetuated. This is shown in some detail in an appendix by the mathematician André Weil.[41] He demonstrates, for instance, that if the following two conditions are satisfied: (1) for every man or woman there is one (and only one) type of marriage he can enter into, and (2) for every individual the type of marriage he can contract depends exclusively on his sex and the type of marriage from which he sprang, then it is not possible that a man be allowed to choose between the daughter of his mother's brother and the daughter of his father's sister. In other words, in such an elementary kinship system either the marriage with the first mentioned type or with the last mentioned type of cousin can be allowed but not both, since otherwise the system (structure) could not be indefinitely perpetuated.

By means of this structural analysis a question which had puzzled many anthropologists is cleared up. Although some previous authors have correctly understood the significance of the rules concerning marriage between cousins, in general they had not been able to explain the distinction, so conspicuous in primitive societies, between the two types of "cross" cousins (daughter of father's sister and daughter of mother's brother). Lévi-Strauss shows that without such distinction elementary kinship systems could not be perpetuated.

Thus, by combining empirical observation and structural analysis Lévi-Strauss has arrived at a comprehensive and original theory of family relations in primitive societies. It is interesting to note that the leading American anthropologist, C. W. M. Hart, has ascribed to *Les structures élémentaires de la parenté* the same fundamental importance for anthropology as Darwin's *The Origin of Species* has for biology.

For our purpose we note that Lévi-Strauss' use of structural analysis by no means precludes, and indeed lends more usefulness to the empirical constructivistic approach to which so many contemporary scientists attribute exclusive validity. *Les structures élémentaires de la parenté* shows the way to, and the great advantage of combining the empirical and mathematical methods under the guidance of a structural description.

7. *The study of the psychology of imagination, restricted to the realm of reflection*[42]

Traditional psychology since August Comte in general, and Dilthey's descriptive psychology, faithful to the current approach, took into account all types of data which seemed relevant to the description of a given situation, without evaluating some of them by pre-established criteria. Thus psychology ignored that conception of research in which the realm of a discipline would be strictly determined by the object, postulated by the objectives of the inquiry and by the methods which they impose.

Jean-Paul Sartre, taking imagination as the object of psychological research, accepts the Cartesian assumption adopted by Husserl that reflective cognition results in certain, indubitable knowledge. While other manners of cognition are dubious, Sartre's approach is determined by the assumption that ". . . he who becomes aware of having an image by an act of reflection cannot deceive himself." [43]

Rejecting the analysis used by traditional psychology, which confused the image itself and the hypothetical theories formulated about its nature, Sartre makes a methodological distinction between two stages of the inquiry. The distinction made between these stages is necessitated by the two mentioned objectives (the image and its nature). Sartre restricts the first stage to the reflective level of psychological activity as the proper domain for studying the origin and development of imagination. By this methodological device Sartre is in a position to introduce, and to elaborate upon throughout the argument, a further distinction of prime importance: that between the product of imagination and the product of perception. Consequently, the first stage of his inquiry is limited to the phenomenological description of the "essence" of the image—the "essence" being inherent in the content of the reflective act. Thus, following this approach, the first task of psychology will be to describe and fix this essence. Once this is accomplished, the inquiry will naturally advance from within the strict limits of the reflective activity and will proceed by drawing hypothetical conclusions about the nature of imagination. Thus, Sartre attempts to combine strict "eidetic" description with theorizing speculation.

The above restriction to the reflective activity, taken as distinct from the perceptive function, and the concentration on *its* products has permitted Sartre to overcome the "illusion of immanence" hitherto dominant both in psychology and philosophy. As a matter of fact, classical philosophers, Hume for instance, have considered the image, inherently a part of consciousness, as something other than consciousness itself. The image, according to classical philosophers, was supposed to be introduced from outside consciousness by the conscious act. In the Humean sense, to have an idea of a chair means nothing more than to "have a chair in consciousness." [44] By Sartre's strict analysis it appears, on the contrary, that an image is only "a certain way in which consciousness presents an object to itself." [45] In the case of the reflective image (in contrast to direct perception), consciousness does not "encounter" the chair. What we find *in* consciousness is not a semblance of the chair, introduced there from outside, but a certain type of synthetic organization of consciousness itself, the very essence of which is the certain manner by which it is related to the external, existing chair. Thus, Sartre's analysis supports the validity of the initial assumption that imagination has its own realm of investigation, where its objects can alone be found in their own nature. This analysis introduces an interesting nuance into classical psychology and philosophy, both of which, according to Sartre, have vitiated the entire issue and confused the object of imagination with that of exterior (outer) perception. An image is nothing but the pure construction of the intentional act; imaginative acts reveal their objects spontaneously, positing them as "nothingness." Here seems to lie the poignant feature of this analysis. As a matter of fact, imagination is creative; its products lack the capacity of perceptual constructions; in crucial opposition to the current view, they do not remain as a passive residuum in our consciousness; they remain there only if perpetuated in their qualitative properties (those of their objects) by the continuous creativity of psychological (intentional) acts.

In the second stage, that of drawing hypothetical conclusions about the nature of imagination which the strict analysis has prepared, Sartre arrives at the most interesting results. As opposed to perception an image does not enrich our knowledge. On the contrary, Sartre attempts to establish, with the help of diagrams as examples, that we can transform a sketch into a rich, meaningful image only by the use of our previous knowledge. In other words, we cannot increase our knowledge by imagination because we need to have knowledge in order to form images. However, the

emergence of images is never the result of chance association. The imaginative attitude seems to be a specially in-
clusive function of the mental life.

But we should never lose sight of the relationship between
imagination and perception. The sharp heterogeneity between them has already been shown in several forms in this
survey. In spite of their intimate interplay this heterogeneity is significantly expressed in the difference of the attitudes which we take before real situations, feelings, and so
on, on the one hand, and before the imaginary ones, on the
other.

It is on this general basis—of the distinction between the
imaginary and the real, with reference to different sources,
natures, and attitudes—that Sartre expects to find a better way
of approaching the explanation of mental disease.

Here we come to what is of greatest interest; in opposition
to the current psychoanalytic view, imagination does not
and cannot attempt to substitute for reality. The schizophrenic's progressively elaborated dream which reaches
large dimensions should not be thought of (as a classical
psychoanalyst would interpret it) as compensating for the
frustration of reality. The dream does not compensate for
experience of reality, and the insanity does not consist
mainly in a reaction to lack of that experience, reality frustration: "If a schizophrenic imagines so many amorous
scenes, it is not only because his real love has been disap-
pointed, but above all, because he is no longer *capable* of
loving." [46]

Thus, the sharp distinction between the two realms—of
imagination and of perception (imaginary and real)—has
become progressively clear as seen in their respective, specific features. This distinction brings to light their mutual
relationship. Although "to posit an image" (a "nothingness") means, for Sartre, to negate the reality—"to construct
an object on the fringe of the whole of the reality," that is,

"holding the reality at a distance"—for this reason the image could only appear on the background of the real world. However, instead of being an activity additional to the perception of the real, as it has been held by classical psychology and philosophy, imagination, on the contrary, constitutes the *meaningfulness* of the real world itself.

8. *Phenomenological trends in psychology, psychopathology, and psychiatry: "experiencing man"*

The most notable import of phenomenology can be observed in psychology, psychiatry and psychopathology as carried out not only by individual workers, but also by groups of researchers and practitioners working closely together in various European countries, particularly in Switzerland, Germany, France and Holland.

It has been recognized in the last few decades that nineteenth-century psychology, searching for *elementary* mental facts (sensations and images) in its atomistic approach to complex mental facts, is unable to explain by the law of association how the elements combine into a unique homogeneous structure. We cannot explain a melody by its component notes, a painting of Rembrandt by the spots of *color* on the canvas, the cathedral of Chartres by the individual stones out of which it is built. Each of these objects possesses a unique structure, which persists if we transpose the shape of the cathedral of Chartres on canvas, Rembrandt's painting in a photograph, or the melody in a different key. The reaction to this atomistic attitude in psychology, seen already in William James' conception of a stream of consciousness, is further exemplified in gestalt psychology, the psychology of behavior, and the descriptive psychology of "understanding." [47] All are more or less characterized by a recurrence of structural considerations, whether they are forms of direct perception, models of behavior, etc. The direct influence of phenomenology on this new direction is indicated by the gestalt psychologist Paul Guillaume, who characterizes this change of perspective in psychology as consisting in a *"simple retour aux faits observés sans prévention, pure description phénoménologique."* [48] The impact of phenomenology is shown also in studies by Jean Piaget (see earlier in this chapter) in the field of child psychology.[49] From the perspective of behavior Erwin Straus should be mentioned for developing a phenomenological study of expression.[50] It was, however, W. Dilthey who, opposing atomistic psychology with the idea of a descriptive psychology, thereby opened a vast field for the application of the Husserlian method. Without denying or refuting the importance of an "objective" approach, he emphasized nevertheless the importance of the "introspective" method. "Since the object of psychology (living man) is always an *entirety,* its method should not be constructive (leading up from a part to the whole) but analytical; not synthetic, but descriptive. Accordingly the aim of psychology cannot be an *explanation* (for explanation reduces into elements); this aim is rather a *description,* an *exposition* or *hermeneusis.* We explain nature, but interior life *(Seelenleben)* we *understand.*" [51] Dilthey opened the way toward descriptive psychology (introspectionistic psychology). This is, however, only the application of the phenomenological method to the psychology of "understanding," which the famous Swiss psychologist and psychiatrist L. Binswanger considers to be one of the chief "revolutions" which psychology and psychiatry have undergone. The Würzburg school of phenomenological psychology must be mentioned first of all in this connection (Hering, Buhler, Katz).[52] In this respect however, the importance of the celebrated German philosophers Max Scheler, A. Pfänder[53] and Karl Jaspers cannot be overlooked.[54] In particular, studies by Scheler and Jaspers have led to a new approach in psychopathology and psychiatry. According to Binswanger, psychopathology is and remains forever an empirical science of facts. As such, however, it needs a phenomenological clarification of its fundamental concepts and thereby a stimulation from phenomenology. Indeed, according to Binswanger, the manifold import of phenomenology for psychopathology has given the latter a new orientation and opened new fields of research.

a. *The concept of inner biography*

Max Scheler had already introduced a distinction between the conception of mental disease in functional terms and the descriptive "content" of the disease. He meant by that, that the content of our mental experience (*seelisches Erlebnis*) is not univocally determined by the organic conditions of its origin, i.e., the processes in the organism or in the brain. Therefore this content cannot be reduced to the causal or parallelistic explanation in functional terms. The brain and nervous system determine the occurrence of functions in which we experience those contents, but not the nature of the contents themselves. Therefore the study of the empirical aspect of mental experience is limited to the observation and statement of the empirical evolution of experience as a unique, historical process. The content of this process itself constitutes, however, a unique mental structure, to which Binswanger, accepting Scheler's distinction, gave the name "inner biography," now widely accepted in psychiatry.[55] While natural science can take care of the first, the second illuminates the connections between the elements of the content of experience "motivating" each other in their factual streamlike progression. These connections, however, are not subject to natural laws but are to be understood as "a unity of meaningful elements motivating each other." [56]

b. *The autonomous source and energy of "higher psychological activities."*

In particular, Max Scheler established two points of major importance for the psychological research which has followed. One of them concerns the source of the so-called "higher psychological activities" like emotions, aesthetic experiences, and spiritual acts referring in general to moral values; the other concerns the energies or forces which engender and nourish these values. In opposition to the Freudian theory of sublimation and its reference of the entire human universe of emotivity and spiritual activity to the drives of the libido, Scheler affirms that, although it must be recognized that a part of the poetic (especially the romantic) sublimation is continuous with the life of passion, it is impossible to extend this concept to all phenomena. So Scheler first of all takes issue with Freud's conception of love. Human love does not merely consist of the sublimation of libido, although it may often happen that the love of daughter for father, or of son for mother, which is grounded in entirely autonomous roots, becomes confused and mixed with other drives of an erotic, sexual nature. In his essay "Love and Hatred," Scheler shows through a phenomenological analysis that there are various kinds of sympathy and love which are not reducible to each other. Freudian analysis completely overlooks this development of new qualities of human feelings, values, aspirations and acts, which can not be understood merely in terms of the gradual and continuous process of natural evolution.[57] For example, it has no adequate explanation of "sacred love," which Scheler analyzes at length. Sacred love, according to Scheler, partakes of the essence of other higher spiritual and emotional acts and is a type of them. This type of love is entirely independent of natural conditions and cannot be produced either through education or conditioning. Its values have no direct, immediate, universally accepted, or practical criteria. On the contrary, its absoluteness and degree of value are determinable exclusively from the very nature of the phenomenon itself. Individuals experiencing this sort of love renounce earthly values for the sake of spiritual ones; they do not do so because of frustration or inhibition, or because life and its goods have no value for them. If such were the case, there would be no sacrifice entailed and consequently no spiritual act achieved. On the contrary, men like Buddha or Saint Francis voluntarily embrace poverty, not as an evil, but as a "radiant bride." Such a free spiritual act cannot be an extension or manifestation of their appreciation of natural life; its completely different nature points to a different source which involves the very structure of the human soul.[58]

Furthermore, Freud, having attempted to explain all "higher qualities" in terms of the libido and its "sublimation," touches on another crucial aspect of human psychological activity. Sublimation is thought to explain the appearance of the spiritual as follows: Once the impulse of the libido is inhibited or frustrated, its energy can be transposed to other objectives of a spiritual nature—for example, art, culture, professional activity. In this perspective all types of love, goodness, higher moral and aesthetic qualities, etc., are merely manifestations of the inhibited libido. But suppose we take Napoleon Bonaparte as an example, says Scheler; according to Freud's theory Bonaparte's genius for military strategy and statesmanship would not have been realized had his union with Josephine Beauharnais been happier than it actually was. But is it not absurd, Scheler asks, to explain military and political aspirations by a tendency to romantic love? It would seem that the only reasonable interpretation of Freudian sublimation is that, "through the act of inhibitions of the libido, the energy which otherwise would be entirely consumed by a limitless submission to the libido will now be directed towards spiritual dispositions and interests." Scheler acknowledges that the entire sum of man's forces is limited and that therefore the use of libidinal energy for one purpose does have some influence upon the energy available for other purposes; he acknowledges also that the drives of the libido are submitted to certain norms and to a certain order. But the specific point of Freud's theory, namely, that there is only *one* source of psychological energy, in which all psychological and spiritual acts partake, is challenged. As a matter of fact Freud's view of the relation between the libido and the higher emotive activities is such that, if it were true, man would be forced to make a tragic choice between primitivism—which, if consistently pursued, would lead him to animality—and the cultivation of spiritual activity, which would lead him to renounce the exercise of central vital forces and the continuity of generation. Scheler brings evidence against the Freudian assumptions. On the one hand, the ascetic life of the monasteries leads neither to extraordinary artistic and spiritual activity nor to neurosis, as Freud would imply. On the other hand, there are innumerable examples of great heights in spiritual—artistic, cultural, etc.—activity attained within a "normal," "natural" life.

In conclusion, Scheler establishes that the "higher qualities"—emotions, spiritual acts, etc.—not only have their own source but also possess their own forces. Otherwise, how could spiritual acts, which need forces in order to overcome the naturalistic tendencies, be performed?

c. *Phenomenological contributions to psychiatric methods*

These distinctions led Binswanger, Jaspers, Bachelard and others to a fundamental conception of man which is larger in scope than the hitherto popular Freudian conception. Instead of seeing man only as a living, *natural* being, man is viewed in his particularity as an *experiencing* being and, in the continuity of his experiencing, as an historically developing *person*. Freud, understanding man as *homo natura* (from which follows his conception of psychiatry as belonging to natural science), correspondingly treats mental diseases by experimental, theoretically constructive, methods. From the word utterances of his patients, understood by the psychiatrist as protocol statements, and from their connections (ramifications), concepts are constructed in view of their systematic relevance to a hypothesis which would explain the symptoms. From the verified hypotheses, theories are constructed stating causes of the symptoms in biological terms. For example, if the father or a father-figure is repeatedly mentioned by the patient among his other utterances the analyst will stop the inquiry into the patient's symptoms, which until now has been conducted in a purely observational spirit, by experimentally making the father element the center of inquiry and seeing all other elements as concentrated around it. The "father complex" in its descriptive unity is now analyzed into its *hypothetical* impact on the patient's life. Further, the analyst proceeds to consider the dynamic aspect of the patient's psychology and its possible biological foundation (this latter inquiry based upon the assumption of a teleology of nature) until he can subsume the individual case under a genus of disease, as for example schizophrenia. The method of inquiry already implies that schizophrenia is understood by reference to a particular theory of natural science (namely, Freud's libido theory).

The phenomenological approach in psychopathology, consistent with its conception of man and its method, does not consider the psychopathological experience of the patient as a species of a psychopathological *genus*. Nor does it reduce it to extrapsychological causes. But it attempts to penetrate, by means of the patient's utterances and their ramifications, into the abnormal mental phenomenon itself. Instead of forming theoretical conclusions, on the basis of the connections between symptoms, about their hypothetical, possibly organic origin, a phenomenological psychiatrist searches only for such characteristics as are immanent in the patient's abnormal experience itself and which reveal his general, abnormal, experiential state. Instead of forming a hypothetical diagnosis based upon attributed predominant importance of some of the elementary symptoms, a phenomenological psychologist aims at perceiving the vast personal background and the entire mental state of the patient without reducing it to theoretically assumed sources and conditions of disease. The Freudian "explanatory" procedure, reducing the symptoms of the disease to their naturalistic conditions within the framework of the libido theory, does not offer clues for determining in what the disease itself consists. A typical example (quoted also by Binswanger) is the attempt made by Bleuler[59] to define the particular character of schizophrenic autism, which states only the conditions under which we talk about autism, but not what autism[60] is. The essential import of phenomenology to psychiatric science consists in multiple, fundamental studies permitting us to determine the exact features of mental diseases such as schizophrenia, etc., in terms of how they manifest themselves in a pre-theoretical description of their phenomenological structures.[61] From a widely developed research we can, in this limited space, only mention the many studies of pathological experiences made by a large group of scholars and practitioners such as E. Kretschmer and H. C. Rühmke, and more recently L. van der Horst, Gurdsdorf and G. Bachelard.[62] However, the analysis of "abnormal" mentality can have the necessary scientific import only if contrasted with a recognition of "normal" mentality. To this effect the phenomenological study of reality made by Hedwig Conrad Martius was of great value.[63] The essential clues to this inquiry are given for the reflection of specialists by the fundamental conception of the world and the even more immediate inquiry into the problems of methods for recognizing the patient's experiences and their multiple forms.

3. Interpretation of results: The irreducible set of categories for a pluralistic universe.

In the perennial inquiry into the nature and laws of the universe the scientist gathers the evidence and the philosopher surveys and interprets it. If we ask the philosopher to interpret the evidence offered by the investigations outlined above, he will doubtless reply that the evidence adduced pertains most conspicuously to the controversy about the categorial structure of the universe—a *pluralistic* conception of the universe seems to be indicated by science. But he will be reminded that adopting or presupposing a categorial position implies commitments and entails consequences which are rarely as "obvious" or as appealing as unexamined premises.

Categorial monism first appeared in the attempts of the pre-Socratics to discover a single material underlying the variety of the world's components. In modern times Spinoza's spiritualism and the recent empirical materialism of logical positivism were likewise committed to conceiving all the components of the universe as completely homogeneous in nature. Thus categorial monism either has to deny the importance of the diversity of things, reduce them to complexes of homogeneous elements, or find itself in the predicament of accounting for the appearance of diversity of things. Cartesian dualism, which attempts to overcome the problems of monism, has difficulties of its own. For if it is necessary to conceive of two categories in order to explain the nature of the universe, it is because from the start we feel constrained to divide everything according to the polarity of two heterogeneous and irreconcilable principles. Thus categorial dualism presupposes in its very origin a dichotomic universe, and the obligation of accounting for the interrelations between the two poles has never been satisfactorily fulfilled.

Can the pluralistic conception of the universe suggested by the phenomenological sciences overcome the difficulties of the traditional categorial positions? In other words, can the pluralistic set of categories account for both the heterogeneity of the components and the pervasive unity of the pattern as a whole? Three aspects of this question will now be discussed in the light of the investigations presented thus far.

1. The demand for a categorial revision stems from the plurality of kinds of residua disclosed by the phenomenological sciences. The work of Ingarden, Malraux, Wellek, Hartmann has shown that cultural monuments must be considered in their own right, as irreducible to creative or responsive psychological processes. In general, we have seen that the uniqueness of man's creative activity cannot be reduced to biological or historical causes. Thus the intelligible content of a cultural phase, although grounded in social, economic, ethnic, and biological conditions, can be shared in common by many individuals, and yet be separable from its material substructure. It has its *own* life and

evolution in history, yet is independent of history—it is "objectified spirit." The specifically *human* is established as exempt from any proposed materialistic reduction.

2. However, the investigation of Piaget, Sartre, and Scheler have revealed that the human, even the mental, is by no means simple. Intelligence, reflective imagination, emotional dimensions, conceptual and sensitive processes, aesthetic feeling and evaluation—these are only a sampling of human functions. Each of them is a stratum *sui generis* of the complete manifestation of man, following its own specific rules. In consequence, philosophical monism explodes into a plurality of irreducible strata which demands a plurality of categories to express them. But, simultaneously, the universe seems to be particularized into many series of discrete components, and we may seem committed to a fragmentation more perplexing than Descartes'.

3. One of the main postulates of metaphysics since Plato and Aristotle has been the presumption that the totality of things in the universe are joined in a continuous chain, from which no link can be missing. This principle of continuity acquired especially strong support in the late nineteenth century from Darwin's theory of evolution, and at the same time the linking agency was given a special interpretation. In the organic world, where the continuity of all creatures seems to form an uninterrupted chain, the agency which accounts for the continuity and unity of progressive development is the organic process, or, more generally, physical interaction or efficient causality. The successful, more developed specimens continue the chain as effects of a natural progression from previous forms of life—their causes. They can be explained in terms of this process of development and the initial organic conditions. Thus the principle of continuity, as interpreted by recent thought in the light of the theory of the origin of species, uncritically opts for a unique linking agency, physical (efficient) causality.

Now only two homogeneous elements can be termed, respectively, cause and effect; no heterogeneous element can be considered a link in the organic chain, and if there appeared some form of life so novel that the process which produced it could not be traced directly, it would be considered an "epiphenomenon." Consequently, the concept of causal continuity in the universe amounts to the reductionist position.

If efficient causality were the only valid way of linking the constituents of the universe, then the heterogenous, distinctive, and irreducible nature of the residua revealed by phenomenological science would allow neither unity nor coherence. If the principle of continuity is to be retained, it needs an entirely new interpretation. It is precisely to this need of a new form of the principle of continuity that the results of Scheler, Binswanger and other phenomenological psychologists and psychiatrists, including Merleau-Ponty, pertain. Man is regarded as the very center of the problem of continuity, for although he is rooted in nature, he extends it and reaches beyond it.

How may we account for the continuity (if any) between these two extremes? From phenomenological psychology comes the evidence that man cannot be identified with a discrete series of symptoms, as proposed in the Freudian orientation, nor with a discrete series of overt actions, as the behaviorism of Watson would have it; for both of these series are conceived as the effects of certain physiological and physical causes. On the contrary, man appears as a distinctively "experiencing" being, so that a mental or spiritual realm, drawing on physiological and physical conditions, must be acknowledged. The continuity depends upon a unique factor: meaning. This continuity could not be held to consist of an interaction of the elements, for the elements are revealed as immaterial and therefore incapable of physical interaction. "Man's destiny" and the "meaning of life" are expressions of this continuity whose successive stages cannot be understood as effects of preceding ones, but which are "motivated" in the way meanings which cannot act on each other can yet have bearing on each other. Their distinctive nature is not caused by the direct action of physiological or other conditions, but is grounded in these and other factors, which, however, have no bearing on the particular form they ultimately assume. Thus the "inner life" of man, the most controversial of realms and the most difficult to establish plausibly, can be seen as it is in itself precisely through this specific new interpretation of continuity based on the new types of connections revealed by phenomenological psychology. The autonomy of man's creations in the arts, society, and culture in general has also been established by reference to non-causal relations, the nature of which varies with the nature of the elements (e.g., functional motivation in the psychology of intelligence). Continuity and unity of the heterogenous components of man and his creations is thus secured.

Falling in line with Descartes, the irreducible specificity of the residua, levels, or strata of man's complex nature is uncompromisingly emphasized. Yet the pitfalls of separating man from nature, mind and body are avoided, for the many strata of man, ranging from the natural to the supernatural, are seen to be complementary and harmonious. Body and mind appear in scientific inquiry not as two separate and opposed segments at the extremes of a series; they are distributed through their various manifestations over the entire range. The division between the "physical" and the "mental" is no sharper than that between two functions of the same reflexive or sensory-motor type. The irreconcilable oppositions of body and mind, man and nature, are eliminated. Merleau-Ponty's philosophical interpretation of behavioral studies is especially pertinent here. No sharp separation of body and mind can be inferred from a series of behavioral manifestations, but only a proportional distribution of some prominent features among all the levels of overt activity. Therefore, it is in terms of these features which are not two but three—the physical, the vital, and the meaningful—that we have to attain a categorial grasp of the world. None of the categories in this set is separate from another; rather, each is represented in all the manifestations of man and only the proportion varies from one level to another.

T W O : *Knowledge of Others*

"What shall we say who have knowledge
Carried to the heart?"

ALLEN TATE

1. The creative function of the existential encounter in the philosophy of Jaspers.

Phenomenology and the so-called "philosophy of existence" have become linked in many ways; in the popular mind they are often confused altogether. Although it does not lie within the scope of our inquiry to disentangle them, a basic understanding of the reasons for their affiliations and divergencies is required. The issue of "the other person" lies at the center of the philosophy of existence and illustrates both its common cause with phenomenology and the distinctive character of each.

The concept of the other person distinguishes contemporary thought from that of previous periods by means of a new philosophical conception which illuminates the spiritual nature of man or, in Kant's terminology, the soul. The concept of the soul, traditionally a mixture of empirical psychological functions, faculties, mystical experience, etc., was completely discredited with the rise of empirical psychology in the middle of the nineteenth century. Understood since Descartes as a substance or the principle of unity of the faculties, the soul was dismissed as mythical by experimental psychology, which worked solely in terms of processes ultimately explicable by physiological and physical causes. The philosophy of existence begins by reinstating the concept of the soul because, it is claimed, neither empirical processes nor mental activities exhaust the truly distinctive spiritual functions.

In so far as the soul, conceived in terms of *Existenz* as irreducible to the purely psychological, is due to a phenomenological orientation and the phenomenological description of man's "inner life," the notion of *Existenz* is a beneficiary of Husserl's phenomenology. However, *Existenz* has been formulated as a specific *dimension* radically distinct from both the natural realm and conceptual structures. Exhibiting no rational structure, it escapes, by its very nature, the purview of the phenomenological method and implies a new type of cognitive insight. The conception of *Existenz* seems to constitute a metaphysical doctrine passing beyond the scope of orthodox Husserlian phenomenology and to develop independently.

It is precisely phenomenology's capability of originating new and diverse doctrines that constitutes its fruitfulness and vast scope. If it were necessary that there be essential affiliations among the many doctrines which have risen to prominence from phenomenological grounds, then phenomenology would be merely a narrow trend of ideas comparable to that of neo-Kantianism. However, if phenomenology consisted only of the application of a strict method, perfectly determinate in scope and interpretation, then its philosophical significance, like that of the program of Unified Science, would soon become sterile. Only new facts could be added. But phenomenology conforms to no program—although unified in its general orientation, it is intrinsically divergent in doctrinal interpretations. The new insights of those doctrines enrich in turn the basic phenomenological orientation and become incorporated into a deeper philosophical view. Keeping in mind, then, the basic affinities and tensions between phenomenology and the philosophy of *Existenz*, we proceed now to examine the most carefully worked out doctrine of *Existenz*, that concerning the other person, which is all the more pertinent to our study for having developed out of scientific research and remained a part of it.

Karl Jaspers writes in the introduction to the series of his philosophical works consisting of metaphysics, epistemology, and logic:[64] "Our point of departure is how man stands and acts towards man as individual towards individual." [65] Jaspers thereby deliberately puts man into the center of philosophical reflection. What do we know about man? The world around us we know by external perception. Our own self, our feelings, and thoughts we know by so-called "internal" or "immanent" experience. But how can we obtain knowledge of other "selves," since what they are is not only what is given to our outer perception—their body, but also this "interior" which is impenetrable to us, given only to their own respective experience? This critical question arose in modern times within the framework of the Cartesian conception of man as composed of two radically different parts: mind and body, *res cogitans* and *res extensa*. Accordingly, an insurmountable distinction between man and fellow man was assumed and the question put forward: "What is the particular act of cognition by which we can approach the 'interior' life of other 'selves'?" In psychology this cognition has been tentatively explained in various ways: by the theory of association, or by analogy to cognition of our own self, or by empathy, the last of which still has adherents. The difficulty in explaining this kind of cognition seems to be particularly acute for psychopathologists when they try to perceive the "inner life" of others in cases of mental disease. The strange emotional expression of a schizophrenic patient does not permit either associative or analogical conclusions with reference to a "normal" observer. It is not only a question of bizarre single elements, but of a vast network of meanings in which the schizophrenic life is shaped, extending to his attitude towards and perception of the exterior world. This pattern of meanings from within which his life arises, proceeds and develops on the most profoundly personal basis. According to the psychological writings of the Swiss philosopher Paul Häberlin, such a pattern constitutes the patient's personality and character. The problem of its recognition is even more important if we consider that psychopathology is supposed to lead from recognition towards therapy, clues for the latter coming from the former.

A step forward in the general method of psychopathology was made by the phenomenological school of psychiatry of L. Binswanger and Karl Jaspers by analyzing and showing what changes mental disease introduces and what it signifies for the mental status of the patient. To quote Binswanger: "The whole spiritual richness of the world (of a schizophrenic patient), the richness of love, beauty, truth, good, the richness of multiformity, growth, and development disappear and what remains is a 'void.' The 'humanity' of man is reduced to the instinctive animal appetite of 'having to fill one's belly.' In this spiritual emptiness he is seized by inexplicable terror or anguish, he is submitted to nightmares and to the strange impact of the world of things and ideas against which he is helpless, even realizing in a second consciousness their real futility.[66] He no longer has the freedom to decide about himself." [67]

By means of the phenomenological method we can describe the strangeness of the schizophrenic's state; however,

Binswanger asks, how can we really recognize and understand the subtle interior mechanics of his development, the sequence of experiences and facts which lead the patient towards this stage of evolution? And this particularly if we consider the fact that the patient is imprisoned within himself, isolated from the human community, and incapable of communicating. The further question arises as to what is essential in man's nature for his growth, fulfillment, and human richness? What is the basis of the freedom which the patient lacks and what is its role in his mental life and in its distortion? All these questions appear central to the psychologist and pathologist if recognition and therapy are to proceed otherwise than blindly. These are, however, metapsychological questions. Obviously, in such an attempt at recognition of the patient's disease, oriented as it is toward helping him in restoring his distorted interior life (*Seelenleben*), the problem of human cognition is strictly connected with the recognition of the relation between that problem and our conception of man and his nature. Can the limited Freudian conception, which views man as perfectly explainable in terms of his biological-physical nature, determine a cognitive approach capable of seizing and understanding the complexity of mental patterns in the fluid reality of real living man? Can the Aristotelian-Cartesian approach taken by science, placing the observer as an objective spectator before a static spectacle of the world as seen from the outside, do justice to his special human plenitude? These are the doubts and questions concerning the approach generally accepted a few decades ago which underlie the new approach toward man's cognition of his fellow men.

Related to this approach is a new conception of man. Contemporary philosophers see both humanity and the world from the point of view of man's particular situation. In this way, such thinkers as Heidegger, Jaspers, Marcel, and Lavelle have abandoned the Cartesian division of man's nature, and have formulated a conception of an integral man that combines the *homo natura* of natural science and experimental techniques with the *homo interior* of Augustine, Pascal, Nietzsche, Kierkegaard. Man is conceived of as not only performing natural functions but also as revealed to himself in a lucid awareness of his destiny, his weakness and fame, his greatness and miseries.

To answer the question of how far modern science recognizes its interest in a clarification of the general conceptions of man, knowledge, and the universe, let us again quote Binswanger, pointing out that the possibility of a creation of a particular mental pattern implies the question of *Lebenszusammenhang,* the way in which life is tied together. This consideration, says Binswanger, leads on the one hand to the question, What is human nature?—on the other hand to the question, How is human nature connected with that which is beyond it? He considers that the answer to this metaphysical question would be the culminating explanation which a psychopathological inquiry into the human "inner self" demands.

Karl Jaspers' philosophical reflections arose from his concern with empirical research in psychiatry.[68] As a famous psychiatrist looking back over half a century of scientific and philosophical research, Jaspers writes: "From the outset I was conscious of the limits of psychology. To protect the patient from the pseudo-knowledge of the doctor I spoke about the infinity [endlessness] and inexhaustibility of every mentally sick patient." [69] The leading idea of his research became, accordingly, the crucial question of methodology: What are the relations between given objects of our cognition and the adequate ways of this cognition itself? What ways of cognition must we recognize in order to do justice to problems and objects with which science and philosophy deal?

In opposition to the opinion held by most psychologists in

the first decades of this century that psychology must employ solely the experimental methods of the natural sciences, Jaspers advances a few empirical considerations resting upon three fundamental, empirical statements:

1. Man in his entirety cannot be objectively (conceptually) known;

2. Cognition is not limited to causal explanation;

3. There are essential aspects of mind which are by their very nature not accessible to experimental methods and cannot be rationally grasped. In this realm, nevertheless, lies the key to the most important riddles of the mind which remain unsolved by natural methods. To such a realm of psychological inquiry belong, according to Jaspers: reactions to experience, development of passions, the origin of error, the inner biography, the individual structure of abnormal personality, etc.

As a result of this greatly enlarged conception of the field of psychology, Jaspers adds to the conventional experimental approach [70] Dilthey's "understanding" of psychological phenomena from "within" and the application of the phenomenological method. However, "understanding" as a method of inquiry into the interconnections of mental life seizes them as if they were static, or as if the mental states were static and conceptually tangible in their entirety. [71] Jaspers insists again and again on the methodological necessity of being aware of this artificial fixation, since his essential conviction is that mental life is dynamic and restless, endless in its dimensions, yet limited in its powers of conceptual cognition. What are these endless dimensions, what is behind conceptual cognition? Indeed, what is man in his entirety?

Here, Jaspers' psychology provokes and finds its adequate counterpart in his philosophy. The basic formulation of the philosophical problems involved arose from Jaspers' concern with psychological methodology culminating in the aforementioned question about the ways in which cognition can do justice to man's totality. Science and natural cognition of the world present us with the world of beings: things and human beings in the conceptual form of "objective cognition." Those beings are thus presented as static in spite of the flux which they undergo. Their static form in cognition is founded both on the nature of conceptual cognition which seizes them statically by means of concepts as well as on the nature of the things of the world whose being consists in "being an object" for the mind. Furthermore, following Kant, Jaspers attributes to the nature of the mind[72] the fact that the empirical world is tangible within a scheme of categories. The nature of things insofar as they are "objects" of conceptual cognition, as Jaspers expressed it, *i.e.*, their mode of being, is to be an object, to have everyday existence—*Dasein*.[73] They are nothing but objects. The static, conceptual form of objects with respect to the mind within the scheme of categories confers on conceptual knowledge the *universally valid objectivity* (in Kant's terminology: *Objektive Gültigkeit*) which is expressed by the fact that we can transfer them directly into language by way of "objective" meanings. In this sense man, understood by psychology as a natural being, is treated by the scientific methods of natural science.

However, Jaspers points out, man seized in static conceptual statements is *understood as* an *object (Dasein)*, an abstract, conceptual product as are all objects treated by natural science, while—and this is his crucial conviction—the *real living* man is *dynamic,* escaping any static determination. Jaspers does not thereby deny that man is primarily a natural being. Man's body can be correctly treated by biological and physiological science. What is more, consciousness as understood by Jaspers is a natural function; he regards it as the "individual reality of existence as experience." [74] In this sense, "consciousness as experience" (*Bewusstsein als Erleben*) together with the human body, constitute the empirical reality of the human being as experiencing human existence, and can correctly be an object of empirical psychology.[75] Following Kant further, Jaspers distinguishes consciousness in yet another sense: as a "universal consciousness, being the universal condition for anything to be an *object* for the knowing subject," [76] which corresponds to Kant's conception of the mind as *unity of apperception*. Such consciousness also being objectifiable, is, in its structure, rules and laws, treated by logic.

For Jaspers, objective cognition can go this far; but here he breaks with the Kantian view which proceeds from transcendental categories *downward* to the phenomena of empirical experience, seeking in what lies *behind* the empirical schemata, the real nature of things. For Jaspers, the ultimate cognition of being has no reference to the realm of empirical existence, that is, to objects of the world. Knowledge of such objects, naïve as well as scientific, for him can be adequate without inquiring concerning "crucial features of being." But being itself is revealed along with the empirical, natural realm, as its necessary encompassing prolongation. Jaspers says: "If I call 'world' the totality of all that is accessible through objective cognition as a cognitive content enforcing its validity on everybody, then the question arises: Does the world exhaust all there is, and is there no other way of cognition that this one exemplified in cognition of the objective world?" [77]

For Jaspers, the crucial philosophical decision lies in the answer to this question: Human beings, as existence, belong to the world. Next, as the counterpart to the world "is what—in the appearance of existence—*is not*, but *can* and *should be* and therefore only time decides if *it is there* and if it is *eternal*. This being I am myself as *Existenz*." [78]

Though he rejects Kantian presuppositions that identify cognition with empirical cognition, Jaspers does deal with metaphysics in the Kantian sense, but in a way which was for Kant cognitively impossible. *Existenz* and *Transcendence*, says Jaspers, are in philosophical language what in "'mythical' language are soul and God." [79]

In point of fact Jaspers agrees with Kant that *Existenz* and *Transcendence* cannot be objectively known, since they are not *objects*, as are the things of the world; nevertheless (according to the distinction introduced by Husserl in contemporary philosophy), not being an *object* organized within categories of objective reality does not exclude something from being an object *for the mind*.* *Existenz is* know-

---

* At this point it seems necessary to make more precise: 1) Jaspers' attitude toward the phenomenological method as far as the cognition of *Existenz* and *Transcendence* is concerned, 2) the meaning which Jaspers confers on the term *Existenz* vs. the current meaning of this term in philosophical tradition. *Ad. 1.* The phenomenological method, as categorial perception of essences, would according to Jaspers' distinction mentioned above, belong to objective cognition; *eidos*, phenomenological essence would represent an objectified rational structure of things and beings. In this sense human *Existenz* has no essence. Nevertheless, Jaspers is using phenomenological method, with this restriction, however, that he emphasizes, as far as *Existenz* and *Transcendence* are concerned, that it is a description of merely provisional and approximately self-fixating structures, ceaselessly fluid by reason of their nature, which consists in the *dynamis* of becoming. It is this process of cognition, which on the one hand informs human becoming and on the other hand resorbs itself in it, that constitutes the basis of *existential reality*. *Ad. 2.* The term *Existenz*, as Jaspers understands it, is obviously to be sharply distinguished from "existence" denoting everyday existence, but also from the term "existence" as understood in the philosophical tradition. Existence (*existentia*) from Aristotle through Scholastic philosophy until recent times was understood as what creates essence in *linea entis*—as an *actus entis;* in other words, as that which brings it about that something *is* in contradistinction to *what* it is. In Jaspers' terminology *Existenz* denotes a specific mode of being including both its *what-there-is* aspect and its *actuality;* this specific mode of being is limited to the human being alone.

There is, however, a tendency on the part of contemporary followers of Thomas Aquinas, such as J. Maritain, to "existentialize" the traditional meaning of "existence," understood as *actus entis*, by endowing it with a "dynamic," intuitive, superrational character; whereas the "orthodox" interpretation of Thomas Aquinas' thought, as represented for example by Del Prado (*De Veritate Fundamentali Philosophiae Christianae*, Fribourg, 1903) or Paul Manser (*Das Wesen des Thomismus*, Fribourg, 1936) understands "existence" as logical, consequently rational and "static." This tendency is related to a

able but in the heterogeneous schemata of *existential* reality.[80] Thus it can be expressed, if only approximatively. We can allude to it by means of objective concepts and approach its cognition, albeit incompletely.[81]

Insofar as the schemata of *existential* reality permit the objective grasp of *Existenz* and *Transcendence,* the latter can constitute, for Jaspers, the subject matter of metaphysics, the science of being.

The whole of being can never be grasped by objective cognition and that is why existence, unsatisfied with objectivity, tends to "transcend."

In the process of "transcending" I realize myself as *Existenz*. In a sense it is man's possibility of decision and choice that transcends the empirical existence of man. *Existenz* is fundamentally this freedom to decide and to choose; as such it is the freedom of the I to be myself. It is through *Existenz* that I become myself, not by the objective cognition of *Existenz*—which is impossible—but by the *elucidation of Existenz*. Here Jaspers' *Elucidation of Existenz* is in contrast with objective, static cognition, first of all by being a process. This process is supposed to be parallel with the process of self-realization (realization of the I), and each motivates the other. *Existenz,* the soul, insists Jaspers, should nevertheless be carefully distinguished from the I.

Jaspers analyzes first the aspects of the empirical ego: starting with the Cartesian "I think," he considers the empirical ego as the fundamental but merely formal aspect of the ego, which does not indicate more than "I know myself as identical with myself in the present and in the sequences

widespread feeling in Europe, which arose from the philosophy of Kierkegaard and the contemporary so-called "philosophers of existence" like Jaspers, G. Marcel, L. Lavelle, etc., that the static conception of being, which prevailed until recent times, is an artificial construct of human understanding.

To avoid *confusio termini,* we shall, with reference to Jaspers' philosophy, use the term *Existenz*.

of time." This consciousness of my *being here* does not contain *what* I am. Furthermore, reflecting upon myself, I seize myself first as a body with all its functions—I am corporeal; however, I am not only my body. Then, I see myself as a social I—I am an existence (*Dasein*) of my social surrounding, but as this alone I am not myself; I can also in self-reflection attempt to identify myself with my achievements; however, I am not only my achievements.

I could accede to myself in what I am only through the past, but the *object* which I construct, considering myself out of my past experiences, evolution, and history, does not realize an absolute identity with myself. Jaspers concludes: in no form of objective thought can I grasp myself entirely. Nevertheless, while from the point of view of the I as empirical existence, I am the concrete *hic* and *nunc* individual which is my first and necessary condition, the factual unfinished character of my picture in time makes me aware of the possibility of becoming *I* in another sense: to become *myself*. This awareness is already a drive towards transcending; it means already the first awareness of *Existenz*—freedom. It is in the process of self-reflection, going from the past history to the actual present, that I elucidate *Existenz*, becoming at the same time more and more aware of what is *right* and *true* with respect to *eternity;* and with respect to eternity, I want them as truthful.[82] When I become *absolutely* responsible and am my own *origin* with the assured self-awareness that with respect to eternity I *know what is true and right,* I pass from the empirical *appearance* of myself to *myself*. The will to create myself is accordingly already freedom—elucidation of *Existenz*. I create myself out of this freedom as an *existential ego,* elucidating *Existenz* in this process. "I am what I become; not what I, as the vital individual, passively grow, but what I, in the midst of self-reflection, gaining my self-reality, want for myself."[83] Here we arrive at the central point of Jaspers' thought:

"This process of becoming *real* [from the preceding stage where I found myself only an *appearance*], by revealing myself (*Offenbar Werden*) does not proceed in an isolated *Existenz*, but with respect to another (to a fellow man). As an isolated *individuum* I am for myself neither revealed (*Offenbar*) nor real." Already as an empirical existence *I am* only by contact and mutual interacting with others. Man is *real* man not by birth but by transmission of human and cultural values which he obtains from his surroundings. The deaf and mute, formerly considered idiots, become fully human after they are taught sign language.

It is only in communication with another that I transcend my empirical ego and elucidate *Existenz*. If the drive and outbreak towards transcending originates from the unsatisfactory finitude of *objectivity*—Jaspers means by objectivity both objective cognition and objective human relations, *i.e.,* "*Dasein* communication," which means life in common with others in social interrelations—the origin of the authentic self is consequently paradoxical: "What it is authentically, it is from itself, but not *only* from itself and with itself." [84] Most of the forms of social relations, as exemplified in the communication of the empirical I, consist either in a mutual understanding of an objective content of thought, or in considering the fellow man as an *object* (empirical, vital being); furthermore, there can be a social communication rooted in common belonging to something encompassing, as, for example, to a social or national group.

The first two of these communications involve man respectively as a formal reason and as a vitality. However, says Jaspers, man is more than this, he is also a *bearer of a content*. This content encompasses the natural drive for simple association with others by the identification of the individual with a meaning by which he finds himself extended towards the world. This is the case with the third social communication, which consists in a common belonging to a common totality. This, however, also has a limit—the totality itself may bring me a meaningful communication, but does not accomplish my identification with myself. In each of those arts of communication I experience a specific satisfaction (*Befriedigung*); in none, however, an absolute. If, however, a communication is under the auspices of some idea, its last limit is *Existenz*. In such a communication I am involved with my whole being and not only with the empirical or social aspect of it. This is *the* communication—existential communication.

Communication is, in Jaspers' conception, a kind of fight, "A fight for sincerity without reserve." By "sincerity without reserve" is meant an offer on the part of two beings to communicate their deepest and most intimate world views, thoughts, intentions, convictions—and this not in order to impose them on the other, but in order to reveal one's most genuine sense of life. However, in the effort to reveal them is contained the effort to realize them for oneself. In this effort to communicate to the other, I realize myself as what I really am in my innermost depths. I realize this deeper sense of myself through what it means to the other and to his own self-revelation, which I meet and in which I participate. Here, revealing to the other means self-becoming. This striving towards the revelation of our deepest convictions to another is not for any other aim than to transcend together the unsatisfactory limitations of objectivity.

The dissatisfaction with the communication of existence constitutes an outbreak towards *Existenz* and towards philosophy which tries to elucidate it. "As all philosophy starts with amazement, with doubt about knowledge of the world, so the elucidation of *Existenz* starts with the experience of dissatisfaction with objective communication," says Jaspers.

Existenz is my essential possibility; its elucidation opens my empirical ego a further encompassing dimension in which the former is contained. *Existenz* is this freedom which enables me to want to realize myself, transforming my *Dasein,* transcending the limits of all objectivity. Elucidation of *Existenz* is a way of encompassing the world towards *Transcendence.* In self-realization the I, rooted in *Dasein,* tends towards *Transcendence*—God. *Transcendence* is not an object; in Jaspers' conception it is to self-realization of the I what *Existenz* is to becoming. Here an additional precision seems necessary. In objective cognition as exemplified in science, psychology, logic, and metaphysics, theoretical objects are thought of. *Existenz* rooted in the factual reality can, as we have said, be thought of approximately in a static way. But we should not lose sight of the fact that it is only a falsifying approximation, since *Existenz* is not an object and therefore cannot be seized by universally valid thought. Elucidation of *Existenz* is meant first of all as a revelation to myself of my encompassing freedom, which may occur while passing from the approximating thought of the possibility of becoming myself to the act of becoming myself. In contradistinction, the truths of objective cognition consist in the adequacy of mentally grasped objects to objects in reality; in the elucidation of *Existenz* "truth will be seized when I myself become it."

This idea is not new. We can forget neither the Socratic conception of knowledge versus virtue, nor can we overlook the high achievements of self-realization in the Neo-Platonic schools of wisdom and in Augustine. This idea often recurs later, e.g., in Nietzsche and Kierkegaard. Finally it has become a very widely shared feature of contemporary philosophy. However, the scientific concern of Jaspers' elaboration, its carefulness and exhaustiveness, brings us back to the scientific source of the controversies and to the demands made by psychiatry and psychology. It is Jaspers' incontestable merit to have clarified philosophically these controversial points and drawn the line between the realms of possible ways of cognition.

To sum up Jaspers' conclusions: *Existenz* (and *Existenz* is at the same time awareness of *Existenz*) is not an experience which can, as an *object,* be treated by experimental psychology. The awareness of *Existenz* (called by Jaspers "absolute consciousness") is again not awareness of *Existenz,* but the "certainty of the being of *Existenz.*" As a mental fact, says Jaspers, it is at the limit of what can become an experienceable reality for empirical psychologists, since it encompasses and at the same time penetrates and transforms all of empirical experience. *"It is,"* says Jaspers, *"this particular dimension of mental life, unperceivable to the psychologist's objectifying sight, which makes everything psychologically knowable particularly unpredictable."* (Italics added.) The same holds for the process of elucidating *Existenz* and for the self-realization of myself: the awareness of this historical process (the same for both) is the awareness of myself, identifying myself with my real self and thereby creating myself in reality.[85] This process "is the most certain and clear in *Existenz,* the least understandable (*unbegreiflich*) for theory." [86]

As a matter of fact, Jaspers specifies, there is an unjustified preconception that awareness can always be seized as a psychological datum, as awareness of an object. Awareness of *Existenz* is, on the contrary, by no means cognition of something, even—metaphysically speaking—of "absolute being." If in philosophy, religion, etc., we talk about *objects* like gods, absolute spirit, being, or about psychological acts in which they can be approached, we seize only what is external, "to know which," says Jaspers, "can be meaningful only as *a means* of coming into real (*eigentlich*) contact with the other by means of my possible awareness of *Existenz:* in *communication,* not in understanding or conceiving, but in realizing (experiencing) the origin while becoming myself." [87]

It is in communication that we can see the basis of the cognition of what cannot be objectively known, of the cognition which is at the same time participation in the other person and realization of myself. Cognition which is based on what is vital and objective penetrates the otherwise inaccessible realms of the basic human freedom. Being general, it finds its accomplishment in the *ultimate* (*Transcendence*) while opening it for the *I* by participation in it with another. Human existence, by its very nature, extends from the physical and vital into the *existential:* into the possible realization of its *authentic* being in *Existenz* tending towards encompassing *Transcendence*. The disruption of this continuity causes the disruption of normal human "experiencing" which manifests itself chiefly by mental disturbances or diseases. The lack of communication, or, more generally speaking, the difficulties, in realizing one's self in *authentic* being, the experience of one's limitations, of being reduced to one's vital and social functions and nothing "beyond" them—in short, the inability to transcend—can, in the light of Jaspers' philosophy, be considered as the fundamental cause of psychological and pathological depressions and despair which lead to disease.[88]

We can already see what Jaspers' philosophy, having arisen from the difficulties encountered in psychological inquiry and its method, contributes towards the clarification of those same difficulties.

1. The first main question of psychiatry is to discover what mental disease consists of and what are its ultimate bases. Jaspers, instead of seeking it in a hypothetically constructed theoretical concept, such as libido or complex, offers a phenomenological description of the *status quo* of the basic abnormality of a mental state. He shows thereby that such states consist principally in a narrowed frame of

mental-spiritual content and its diminished dynamism, in the lack of inner freedom, in the lack of a deeper sense of life (*Existenz*).

2. Concerning the method of recognition of others' states of mind, Jaspers emphasizes that in order to recognize others' inner selves it is not sufficient to perceive and objectify statically, whether by empirical methods or by phenomenological "understanding." The restless, genetically infinite, richness of other selves cannot be entirely grasped conceptually. It can, however, be participated in, not only by empathy, which consists in a *reflecting* in our own self of the state of the other self, but chiefly in "communication," which means a mutual *creation*.

3. Communication constitutes a genetic aspect of cognition (or rather a cognition of the specifically genetic in the mental): *cognition in becoming,* the knower and the known in the relation of a mutual self-creation, self-realization towards a higher spiritual *telos-Transcendence*. In this sense the process of recognition means an already "therapeutic" process. It is in this sense that we could perhaps understand the basis of a successful psychiatric "transference."

Furthermore, we have seen the methodological foundation which Jaspers gave to the conception, introduced by Binswanger and since predominant in psychiatry, of man as an experiencing (and not merely naturally functioning) being, and the definition of the task of psychiatry as essentially devoted to the inquiry into the inner biography. On the other hand, his philosophy of self-realization in *Existenz* with its heights and depths clarifies the spiritual nature of the inner biography itself, the situations in which it flourishes and its low points as exhibited in mental disease. Finally, responding to Binswanger's demand, Jaspers' philosophy of the continuity between the empirical world and the spiritual, encompassing *Transcendence,* gives to the science of man a framework and horizon.

2. The new perspective in the social sciences.

The foregoing analysis of Jaspers' conception of the existential encounter shows the metaphysical depth with which the problem of the other person has been treated in contemporary philosophy. In some sciences, such as psychology and psychopathology, its full metaphysical significance has been crucially instrumental.[89] In other types of research, particularly in sociology, the concept of the encounter with the other person, stripped of its more speculative aspects, has made interpretations possible which offer a novel perspective leading to a basic revision of previous theories.

The social sciences, as distinct scholarly pursuits, are relatively young, dating back no farther than the work of Auguste Comte in the middle of the nineteenth century. In their early development they benefited from the current philosophical and historically conditioned concepts of society, the state, and the individual. However, the new sciences were also hindered by the perpetuation of questionable oppositions such as that between society and the individual: the assumption was that society was an autocratic governor, the individual an isolated social atom struggling for the rights due him. This opposition between society and the individual becomes suspect in the light of the recognition of the creative function of knowing another person, and the perspective in social investigations is radically changed. The state, society, and moral institutions are no longer considered as forms external to man; on the contrary, they are envisaged in terms of social relations, relations among the individuals forming them. The decisive change in the concept of society is due not only to the recognition of the creative role of knowing another person but also to analysis of social relations by phenomenological techniques. Social relations are treated neither from the

mystical point of view nor from the utilitarian and biological point of view, but are examined at the various distinctive levels of specifically human nature. With this new
perspective, sociological research, oriented by phenomenology,
is broadening the application of its techniques.

In the following sections, we shall discuss the existential
(spiritual) commitments involved in human relations, e.g.,
in the context of the family. Furthermore, the consciousness
of human community, the "us," will be shown to be an
equally basic psychological phenomenon and a fundamental
constituent of the human community; social forms and structures will be shown, with reference to the forms of "sociability," to be subjectively grounded, yet distinctive. The
social institutions of justice will be seen to refer to unchangeable principles rooted in the social acts of the individual, acts which have an intrinsic orientation to another person. In economic research we shall see a pattern
of invariant economic types, first based on individual "plans"
and then referring to an inter-individual exchange system.
Finally, the inquiry into rational behavior will be brought
back to the fundamental pre-reflective nature of human
consciousness which, even at that most primitive level of
man, appears to be motivated to reach beyond itself by its
concern with another person.

1. *The encounter with the other in human relations*

The cognition of others is treated by the French philosopher
Gabriel Marcel. It was he, as a matter of fact, who first
focused the attention of contemporary philosophy on this
problem, which has since been taken up by various thinkers.
Jaspers' general conception of the encounter with the
other, elaborated much later, coincides with the ideas of

Marcel. In terms of this encounter Marcel explains the most complex and subtle human relations.

The consciousness of others is, for Marcel, an elemental constituent of our being, for it is a necessary condition of the consciousness of the self.[90] Any affirmation about self, such as "I am tired," supposes a dialogue of this type: "Somebody is tired. Who? I." This dialogue would be meaningless if the word "I" were not addressed to somebody else, for whom we are "the other." The "ego" exists only in relation to others, almost in opposition to others, as is shown clearly in children's reactions. A child gives flowers to his mother. "I picked them for you," he says, thus excluding all others from his mother's thoughts.[91] The same exaltation of self in reference to others is found in the pride of the adult trying to make others acknowledge his wonderful qualities. Such acknowledgment is necessary if he is to transform his bare feeling of existence into a consciousness of self. All egocentric preoccupations act as a screen between us and others, for the other person is then treated only as an object. We can reach a complete consciousness of our "ego" only by meeting the other man beyond the level where he treats us as an object. It is our only chance to get rid of the obsession of the "ego" and discover the legitimate love we can have for ourselves. For Marcel, the only necessary condition for such an encounter is the readiness of the two persons, which alone permits of a living exchange. Encounter is a *co-presence*. This presence is not an object and cannot be "realized"; it can only be welcomed or refused; it is an intersubjectivity, a communion.

For Marcel, this intersubjectivity, this communion, is love. Consequently it cannot be defined, but we can describe some of its conditions and requirements. The first condition for love as well as for friendship is a mutual invocation: "Be with me." This reciprocal invocation is the very type of vocation which leads, if answered by a complete engagement and an authentic faithfulness, to "being." Such a communion is reached in married love, when wife and husband swear to be faithful to one another. Its consequence is an inner influx which breaks down the barriers of egotism which kept us prisoners, and becomes a source of life, leading us to further creative activity. Faithfulness also plays a rôle at the ontological level insofar as it multiplies and deepens the consequences of the initial engagement.[92] We are all divided between two wills, one oriented toward egotism and never satisfied, the other tending toward communion and able to lead toward peace and joy. Faithfulness is the spontaneous and continually renewed choice of the second tendency. The perfection of being depends upon that of the freely accepted and ratified communion in love. It is not enough to conceptualize it, or even to accept it; one must also participate in it. What are the types and dimensions of this participation? For Marcel, charity is its dimension; love, family, parenthood and filiation constitute its types. These essential human relations, involving our entire being, create us.

The family, for example, does not exist in any true sense if it is reduced to the reality of an institution which can be entirely understood by positive science. The family—its authentic, spiritual reality—is rooted in existential participation which may and should become a communion in being, a communion which demands a commitment without which we could not be living persons but merely abstract concepts.[93] The mystery of the family emerges from the infinite net of engagements of our being, which we can accept or refuse. Starting with the most concrete ties which, as a member of a family, involve us in attachment to a certain permanent home, its character, way of life, and spirit, we evolve within a subtle net of spiritual inheritance, of stories from the past, examples, models, from which we emerge as a link in a continuous chain, as a step in a hierarchy in which we are caught by our origin, in which we engage ourselves, in which we find ourselves. This hierarchical structure is made up of the relations among the members of a living group, their relations and those which they entertain by their appreciative evaluation of other generations. Here the key concept is that of our relation to the other: We would not give ourselves, or situate ourselves, *in* the family without *recognizing* ourselves as belonging to its spirit, rules, tradition. It is through this act of evaluative recognition of its values that we shape ourselves as belonging to it. Through this and other similar channels we receive the spiritual heritage of our predecessors. To teach a child to understand appreciatively a certain familial notion, for example of honor, means to invite him to realize it personally in his own life. Gratitude is related to the act of recognition. Receiving the spiritual heritage with gratitude means a *creative faithfulness*. Creative faithfulness makes me inherit a tradition by incarnating the universal values of the tradition in my particular circumstances.

In the inverse direction, there is another equally essential relation for the family: we are also constituted by our successors, we participate in them as they participate in us, we are "consubstantial."

As filiation does not consist either in the biological or the social status but in these more complex relationships, so also with marriage and parenthood.[94]

The family is not the only community which represents *our self-creative commitment* to association with others. Charity, faithfulness, recognition, spiritual inheritance of a universal mission, work in all human groups, cultural, professional, political and others. These commitments act to prevent small communities from becoming closed and ingrown and thereby obstacles to a vaster union which will involve the whole of mankind. They also create the historical, social and cultural type of any particular epoch.

The cognition of others, which Jaspers has put at the center of his philosophy, constitutes within the general framework of contemporary philosophical, psychological and literary thought a new and stimulating insight. The action of man upon man, resulting in a reciprocal shaping, is a central philosophical idea of the above-mentioned philosophers; moreover, cognition understood as a *co-creativity, co-nascere,* is to be found also in the literary realm, as for example, in Paul Claudel's famous *Art Poetic.*[95]

The knowledge of others receives a thorough treatment by Maxime Chastaing.[96] The results of a similar inquiry conducted by the Belgian philosopher, Maurice Nédoncelle, show that there is no limit between the I and the fellow man, that consequently the Other does not form a borderline for my own self, but is rather its source; this constitutes a central idea of his philosophy of love.[97]

2. *The inter-mental approach in sociology*

The problem of the Other expresses itself in an "inter-mental" approach of psychological phenomena and has brought about a change of perspective in sociology. Unlike nineteenth-century sociology, which had an "atomistic" conception and saw in society a clash between the rights of the individual and the state considered as a group of individuals, contemporary sociology denies that such an opposition exists.[98] An individual's very nature embodies a social structure, which means that he is necessarily related to his fellow man. Individuals create one another as social beings. The type of society they originate depends upon the modes of interdependence. Consequently, in such an integrated structure of society, as G. Gurvitch expresses it, there is no longer a question of relations between individuals and society, radically opposed to each other.[99]

Perhaps the most significant contribution to sociology was made by Max Scheler, who followed Husserl. Husserl had attempted in the *Kartesianische Meditationen*[100] to overcome the danger of solipsism by establishing an interior relation between the I and the thou, in which the evidence of the thou is not only indispensable for, but even prior to, the cognition of ourselves. Scheler (in opposition to classical sociology) affirms that the various forms of social unity correspond to various forms of inter-individual communication. He thereby shifts the locus of investigation. Instead of considering multiple human emotive relations as a social product, he goes into the nature of man to explain the social, and considers emotivity in the form of sympathy a fundamental condition of all communication and sociability. With reference to specific kinds of emotivity: sympathy, identification, a simple "feeling together," etc., he distinguishes parallel forms of social unity. The highest form of sociability is, for him, that of spiritual solidarity, as for example in a church or a nation.

This shifting of emphasis (the individual becomes the key to the social) has given rise to a phenomenological sociology. A. Vierkant, under the influence of Scheler, has reinterpreted the prephenomenological conception of the sociology of relations as referring to a fundamental category of the notion of community which is specifically characterized by an individual consciousness of the "us" (*Wir-Bewusstsein*).[101] In this consciousness the I retreats before the feeling of our intimate belonging to a group. This category defines itself in terms of relations emerging from the innate disposition of all humankind. These relations can be grasped in a phenomenological intuition, as for example the feeling of self, the will to power, the tendency to subordination, etc.

It is in these tendencies or dispositions that community relations are grounded. Thereby the organic conception of the community is abandoned and, as also in Scheler's view, the community is conceived as purely spiritual.

Theodor Litt, using also this phenomenological approach, has come to the conclusion that psychology and sociology have as their common object "lived experience." In other words, since the community is an expression of a form of consciousness and of the experience of the I, and both particularize themselves in individual forms through experienced reality, there are only two possible perspectives. In one the accent is put on sociability (as a form of consciousness), in the other the accent is put on the individual experience.[102] The relation to *the Other* is constitutive of the *I* itself, since one cannot grasp one's relation to another except from one's own point of view; at the same time one cannot grasp oneself except as one of the terms of relation with another person. In other words, this relation corresponds to the I as a "center of life" and as a "center of vital perspective." However, the real, complete, social relationship emerges only with the coming of a third person on the scene. This completes the "closed circle" of the "reciprocity of perspectives," and defines the social relation.

For Th. Geiger there exists really only one social form, namely, that of the group; the community is a solidarity in the consciousness of "us" interpreted metaphysically as "a fusion of men in being"; the personal contacts in which it is grounded can be formulated as "the relations between Me and Thee within the Us." [103]

Although the inter-mental approach was at first attacked by non-phenomenologically oriented scholars, it has more and more gained acceptance. Even Durkheim, its strongest opponent, admitted finally that collective representations are the product of an immense cooperation, which extends not only in space but in time as well; to produce such representations, many minds working through countless generations have combined their ideas, sentiments, experience and

knowledge.[104] Moreover, E. Dupréel as early as 1912 defined sociology as a study, not of society, but of social relations. Later on, in his *Sociologie Générale,* Dupréel explained the relations characteristic of the community in
terms of specific dispositions of human beings.[105]

3. *The sociological synthesis of
phenomenological methods*

The most representative effort, however, is that of G. Gurvitch, the prominent French sociologist. Gurvitch first of
all makes a distinction between social structures and forms
of sociability.[106] Against the tendency to reduce a multiplicity
of perspectives to a single one, Gurvitch develops an irreducible pluralism of the forms of sociability. Whereas by a
social structure is meant the form of a complete, globally
considered society, the forms of sociability represent the
multiple ways in which integration into the whole of a social
structure is possible. They represent types of particular social
groups constituting the complete society. The study of these
forms of sociability he calls "microsociology," parallel to
microphysics, etc. Following the phenomenological intuition
of irreducible residua, or phenomena organized in stratified
structures, Gurvitch distinguishes various strata of forms of
sociability along a vertical direction "in depth." Although
there is an interplay, even a sort of motivation, between the
various strata, nevertheless it appears that they are irreducible
to each other as effects to causes. More precisely, there is an
interplay between the psychological level of a *collective consciousness* and the stratum of *spontaneous sociability,* which
lies beneath the symbols and institutions that together constitute an *organized sociability.* However, in spite of the fact
that various forms of spontaneous sociability refer directly
to the collective psychology, no causation can be inferred.

Overcoming the evolutionary approach, only a reciprocal interaction in terms of mutual motivation is established.

4. A priori foundation of civil law

Special attention should be devoted to an outstanding, and yet little known, attempt at laying down the *a priori* foundations for legal doctrine. In 1913, independently and in advance of all the mentioned developments, Husserl's disciple, Adolf Reinach, had already formulated a theory of civil law, consisting of specific, irreducible "social acts," which attempted to clarify the very puzzling question of the nature and origin of the "ties" (*Bindungen*) contained in the basic legal notions of promise, claim, and commitment, as well as the legal maxims.[107]

Reinach takes as a starting point the nature of positive law, on the one hand, and the nominalistic (Hume), psychologistic (Th. Lipps), and other attempts to explain the origin and nature of positive law, on the other.

Positive law remains in a perpetual flux of development and change which goes along with the prevailing moral opinions of a given epoch and the ever changing economic needs and circumstances. For instance, the legal maxim saying that claims to a thing or service can be ceded to a third person by the creditor without the consent of the debtor, is a proposition of modern law which had no validity in earlier periods of law. Its formulation and present validity seem to be the result of specific economic needs.

Considered in this light, positive law seems to be created by the legal factors mentioned above in order to fulfill needs of the time. During that period its rules and notions might be "correct," while at another time an opposite rule might appear "correct." According to this view it would be inappropriate to think of the intrinsic or objective "truth" or "falsity" of a given maxim or legal notion. However, quite often in jurisprudence reference is made to rules that, without belonging to the written law, "are evident in themselves" or "follow from the nature of the case." It is to this "self-evident" nature of legal formations that Reinach refers, while opposing the then—and now—current tendency to understand the propositions and notions of positive law in terms of economic and social circumstances, or at the utmost, in terms of psychological acts. Reinach's thesis, which will be discussed, is that legal notions, maxims, and laws are based on specifically legal formations or structures, which possess a being independent of whether positive law has discovered them or not. Positive law *discovers* them, but does not *produce* them. Without establishing the existence and nature of such ultimate structures and their connections, positive law remains utterly inexplicable in its nature and development.

Reinach's theory of irreducible legal formations is based on a twofold distinction. First of all, he introduces an important refinement into Husserl's theory of conscious acts by making a distinction between intentional and "spontaneous" acts. The second distinction concerns these spontaneous acts. It differentiates between "inner experiences" and "social acts." In order to see this, let us follow Reinach's thought through a problem in which he introduces us to the new realm of legal inquiry.

A man makes a promise to another. From this action a singular effect emerges, a quite different effect than if a man gives information to another or makes a request: "The promise creates a specific 'tie' between two persons, in consequence of which . . . one can claim something from the other, and the other commits himself to do, or to give, it." [108] This "tie" seems to be a result, a product, of the uttered promise. According to its very nature, this claim-commitment "tie" extends over a period of time; nevertheless, it possesses an inherent tendency to come to dissolution, to an end. The very nature of this "tie" suggests various ways by which it may come to dissolution: for example, the content of the promise may be fulfilled; the recipient of the promise may resign his claim; or he who promised may revoke the promise; and so on. The question arises, What are these curious entities of claim and commitment which come into being when the promise is made? Had these entities not possessed a distinct being, they could not be annihilated by fulfillment, resignation, or revocation. Obviously, they cannot be of a physical nature.

On the other hand, as against attempts made, for instance, by Th. Lipps, to understand these entities as psychical acts of those persons who enter into the claim-commitment relation, we see that, while psychical experiences constantly change, a legal claim-commitment tie can remain unchanged throughout years.

Moreover, claims and commitments are legally valid and remain identical while the people involved are not actually experiencing anything, as for instance, in sleep. They remain identical while the persons involved cannot even remember having made them, as for example, in cases of amnesia, or even if they deny them, because of some complicated psychological processes. Now, falling in line with Hume on this point, Reinach nevertheless refutes the nominalistic conception of Hume. To the conception of legal maxims and notions as unchangeable, permanent, autonomous, and independent entities—in the sense of timeless mathematical objects—Reinach opposes the temporal character of the claim and commitment, their formation, their temporary persistence in being, and their later complete annihilation. By an analysis of their nature we can, however, succeed in establishing their specific status among other types of beings.

In the first place, claim and commitment presuppose a

subject, a "bearer" (*Träger*). This subject—in contrast to experiences which animals also have—can only be a *person* whose claim or commitment they are. In the second place, they possess a *content* which establishes what someone has a claim to, or has committed himself to, and on what conditions. The content always refers to the future behavior of the subject. In the third place, each commitment and each claim also has, not only a bearer, but an "addressee"; by their very nature they point to someone other than the bearing subject, a "counterpart" (*Gegner*). Commitment presupposes someone with respect to whom it exists. Indeed commitment reveals a very compact structure: the counterpart of the commitment is simultaneously the bearer of the claim. This claim has a content identical to that of the commitment. In its turn, the claim points necessarily to the counterpart, who is simultaneously the bearer of the commitment. In these terms a specific correlation is established between claim and commitment: an identity of content and a mutual, strictly interwoven, legal connection between being a bearer and being a counterpart.[109]

Nevertheless, there still remains the possibility of understanding this structure in terms of relations between psychological acts performed on the side of the "bearer" and the counterpart. In order to show the fallaciousness of this possibility and to reveal the specific status of this legal formation, we need to take advantage of the two aforementioned distinctions, by which Reinach amplifies Husserl's theory of the intentionality of consciousness.

In opposition to intentional experiences, such as hatred or sadness, which can force themselves upon the experiencing subject, Reinach distinguishes among experiences which are not only merely intentional but in addition emerge from a special mental attitude of the subject or "I." Examples of such acts—which, in distinction to the merely intentional, Reinach calls "spontaneous acts," or "spontaneous experiences"—would be the act of making a decision (in opposition to the state of mind which entertains a decision), performing an act of preference (in opposition to the passive disposition of a preference once established), the act of asking, ordering, and so on.

Here again further distinctions must be made. There is a difference between the act of making a decision and of giving an order: the first—apart from its intentional orientation towards the object of decision—remains within the subject, is an "interior" one; the second, on the contrary—apart from its intentional pointing towards the content, the object of the order—points to a *second subject*. The second subject is the person to whom the order is directed. Furthermore, among acts "oriented towards other persons" (*fremdpersonal*), some—for instance, the act of giving an order—are distinct because of their specific dependence upon that other subject: *they must be received by the Other* (*vernehmungsbedürftig*) in order to come into existence themselves.[110] Such acts, which are not only spontaneous (and intentional) but also oriented towards other persons who must necessarily receive them, constitute according to Reinach a special, distinct type of act. These acts define societal life and development, and therefore Reinach calls them "social acts."

At this point, Reinach renders to the psychological interpretations their limited due: for instance, an order presupposes an individual experience, a psychological "inner experience." An order presupposes not only an act of desire but also of will performed by the person giving the order. Furthermore, these "inner experiences" modify the social acts in various ways. On the one hand, without the "real" experience of assurance, wish, or will there can be only a pseudo-request, a pseudo-order, a pseudo-promise (*Scheinbitte, Scheinbefehl, Scheinversprechen*), and so on. On the other hand, there can be an order, a request, and so on, at large, or a conditional one. The power of action of a conditional social act refers to something which will occur after the condition is fulfilled.

However, the fact that social acts are rooted in individual psychological acts does not mean that they are identical with, or explicable by them. On the contrary, these and several other possible modifications of social acts, resulting from their origin in individual acts, reveal even more clearly how these modifications refer to the specific structures of which social acts consist, independent of all empirical facts and statements.

The most revealing modification of social acts is evidenced by social acts performed "on behalf of" (*in Vertretung*). For example, to give an order, information, and so on, "in the name of someone else," is to bring about a social act consisting of a specific, strictly determined structure. This structure involves the bearer and the counterpart in their specific relationship; also, it involves the possibilities of its existence and its dissolution. This structure is exactly "the same" as if the act were performed by the individual entering into this structure himself; however, the experiential act in which this structure is rooted (desire, will, and so on) is performed, not by the authentic, "true," bearer of the act, but by someone else. While the actual performer remains entirely outside the structure, the social act functions as if performed by the authentic bearer. How the structures of social acts, though rooted in individual experience, constitute specific formations constructed upon this experience should thus be evident. These formations exhibit their own autonomous nature and internal laws.

The fundamental legal notions and maxims can be referred to the specific nature of social acts. For instance, a legal promise may seem to be a social act. It presupposes the inner experience of will, not by the addressed person but by the promising one, that something will be accomplished.[111]

Nevertheless, the promise is neither an act of will nor a declaration (as some pretend) of an act of will. Although its declaration is necessary in order to make it a promise,[112] a legal promise is still "an independent, spontaneous act, which while pointing to the outside, comes to an exterior manifestation." [113] The specific tie resulting from a given promise, which consists of the inner mechanism of the claim-commitment structure, is now revealed to consist of intuitively perceivable, essential connections between the specific elements of the whole formation. Reinach offers numerous examples of such structural explanations of legal notions which are distinct and independent in their nature, even though rooted in psychological acts. For instance, obligation consists of the entire relation founded on the promise-claim-commitment structure. A further example may be seen in the notion of the contract which denotes a structure constituted in terms of mutual social acts of agreement. Reinach has thus established the distinct, independent, and indestructibly ultimate nature of legal formations, consisting of irreducible legal elements and the necessary connections among them. Consequently, he considers these legal formations as sets of possibilities and norms for all empirically conceivable legal notions and rules. Furthermore, he considers them as a basis for further inquiry into normative and *a priori* legal rights and obligations (for example, with regard to property) and legal laws (for example, with regard to legal ceding).

In the light of this inquiry the validity of the positive law, changeable as it may be in its empirical legal statements, notions, and maxims can definitely be seen as a temporary recognition of some of the permanent, *a priori* (independent of all experience) legal formations. The legal formations can sometimes be empirically recognized and at other times entirely ignored. But the internal consistency of the identified legal maxims, notions, and their property of being "correct" refer to the independent legal formations. Thus, legal formations play the role of unchangeable and indestructible norms which prescribe for the empirical concretions their principles and the limits of their possibilities.

5. *Invariant types of economic systems*[114]

Late in the nineteenth century two approaches to the explanation of economic life and its laws came to occupy leading positions. The historical school, headed by Schmoller in Germany, considered the economic development of a country in a given period as an integral part of the general historical development and claimed that such development can only be understood when it proceeds from a knowledge of the social, political and intellectual history of the time. Consequently the method of economic research should follow the course of historical events, establishing hypothetical relations among the mentioned realms. The opponents of the historical school, on the contrary, considered economics to be a deductive science which could derive a comprehensive theory on the basis of a strictly limited number of universally applicable assumptions, in particular the principles of marginal utility, and claimed that historical methods "do not enable us to explain the interrelationships within an economic system, i.e., do not allow us to trace observed economic facts to their economic causes." [115] For instance, the historical school could not explain the causes of economic events such as the German inflation after World War I. As far as the methods of the theoretical approach are concerned, revolutionary events in history seemed to overthrow entirely the applicability of any hypothetical, abstract theory.

According to F. A. Lutz, in his introduction to the major work of the noted economist Walter Eucken, the main question which Eucken proposes to answer, challenging the current trends, is: "What is required for a full understanding of economic reality anywhere and at any time?" [116] Eucken contends that, since a general interpretation of historical events leads necessarily to some ideology as a clue, the historical explanation of economic systems amounts, in point of fact, to an ideological explanation. As such, it can also become a political weapon. For example, "in the course of every serious depression the old, long-credited notion that too much of everything is being produced, in one country or in the world, is spread by prejudiced writers in order to create opinion in favor of a planned restriction of production." [117]

However, Eucken also strongly opposes the "conceptual" procedure—a more recent development of the theoretical school—which, as interpolated by O. Spann, seems to base its foundation on a direct analysis of "essences." Although Spann's demand for a "necessary, strictly unequivocal structure" of the economic reality (*Notwendingkeit, strenge Eindeutigkeit, Gesetzmässigkeit*) at which we can arrive only by the analysis of "essential natures" of economic factors, brought forward in the time of historicism and psychologism, suggests that he was strongly influenced by Husserl's *Logical Investigations,* his inquiry amounts in reality to a formal analysis of concepts.[118] Eucken objects that the analysis of "formalists" like Spann are made without "so much as a glance at the facts." [119]

The current approaches to economics fail to offer a solution to the "Great Antinomy." This Great Antinomy consists, according to Eucken, in the difficulty of explaining simultaneously the flux of the changing economic process and the necessary, invariant connections among its components. The theoretical approach fails because of its strictly rational, axiomatic procedure, which deserts facts; but so does the empirical method, if practiced rigorously.

Eucken approaches this difficulty by elaborating in an original way the ideal, invariant aspects of economic reality as contained within the factual context of economic life, and the factual aspects of economic problems as based upon ideal structures. To understand economics is to explain the economic process and this has to be done by relying upon facts, since economics is an empirical science; but at the same time one must grasp permanent structural interrelations among them, since this explanation should be valid "in any time and any society."

Although he opposes Spann's too literal understanding of an *a priori,* "essential" analysis, Eucken seems, as much in his general aim and conception of economic study as in his detailed methodological devices, to be profoundly indebted to Husserl, whom he quotes on various accounts. He refers, in the first place, to Husserl's fundamental conception of empirical experience as a starting point for empirical science and its phenomenological treatment. If scientific knowledge ought to consist in an "essential" grasp of economic phenomena, these essences of foreign exchange, rise in prices and wages, changes in production, foreign trade relations, etc., are not perceived separately from actual economic realities. On the contrary, a tremendous amount of observation of these realities is needed in order to arrive at their essential structures. However, empiricists, believing that these structural connections between facts can be discovered simply by describing facts, will fail to understand concrete economic life and its interrelationships. No connections between the facts can be established—for instance, out of all the possible data about prices, wages, monetary circulation and foreign trade, national debt, industrial and agricultural production, etc., in America—that could lead in the end to a theory explaining the depreciation of the dollar during and after the American Civil War. The purely empirical procedure cannot advance beyond a collection of unanalyzed facts, and does not explain how each economic fact hangs together with others as a whole in the economic process. Therefore the method adopted by Eucken falls in line with phenomenology, aiming first at an exact description on the basis of vast amounts of factual data of the ideal structures of economic life, which he distinguishes in terms of "ideal types." [120] Secondly, through a systematic survey of all these individual types as they occur in various periods of human history—for instance, some which may have been extant in ancient Egypt but unknown in Greece, others which may have existed in the Middle Ages but are entirely out of place in the modern economy, etc.,—Eucken aims at arriving at a fundamental, universal structure of economic life as an invariant basis of all past, present and possible economic systems, events and processes.

If we pursue in detail the investigation of economic reality, we will arrive at a basic statement at the very outset of the inquiry. If we ask why the peasant is plowing a field today, the answer is "because it is a part of his economic plan." So may we ask, "Why is the agricultural worker plowing on a larger farm?" and arrive at the answer: "Because of the economic plan of the estate manager." Or, "Why does the housewife buy an ample provision of fruit today?" "Because it is part of her economic plan." Similarly, if administrators of some medieval monastery planted a large number of fruit trees of a special kind at a particular time, or the controller of the Egyptian temple economy assigned a large sum of money for a new temple, they acted on the basis of their economic plans.[121]

Eucken is led by these observations to ascertain a universal form for all economic life: "At all times and places man's economic life consists of forming and carrying out economic plans. All economic action rests on plans. The precision and the temporal range of the plans are very different with different people. . . ." But none of man's economic actions are without a plan.[122] The formation of the individual plan becomes the first objective of Eucken's further investigation with a view to discovering the "pure structural elements out of which all actual economic units or structures are built up." [123] In fact, he establishes two "pure elemental forms" to be found in whatever economic process in history we examine; in short, two ideal types of economic systems. The first of them is the *centrally directed economy,* and the second, opposed to the first, is the *exchange economy.* Eucken asserts: "No other types of economic system, or even traces of others—besides these two—are to be found in economic reality past or present. It is hardly conceivable that others can be found." [124]

The centrally directed economy has two main features. First, the distribution of consumers' goods is handled through administration according to directives from a central authority. Whether the exchange of consumers' goods is entirely prohibited among the consumers, or is allowed within some limits, the result is that the entire everyday economic life of the community is under the control and follows the plan of a central authority. Even if it appears that, through some extent of allowed exchange, the autonomy of the single planner is limited by the expression of individual needs and plans through individual demands, this permissiveness is so negligible that it does not truly affect the system of centrally directed economy. Actually, the propaganda pressure exercised by the central authority and the overwhelming part played on the markets by the decisions of the central authority will subordinate the individual plans to those of the authority.

Nevertheless, faced by individual economic plans, the central authority may deal with them in either of two ways. It may attempt to exclude any influence of the individual plans on its own, or it may consider the assertion of individual plans as an index of the needs of the population, and, in drawing up its plan, take into account the individual plans. In the second case we reach the limits of what can be defined as a central economy, and pass over into a form of *exchange economy*. "An exchange economy of pure type," says Eucken, "is made up of firms and households which are in exchange with one another." [125] Opposed to the centrally oriented economy, where the economic process of the community is entirely determined and therefore forms a complete plan, in the exchange economy, the individual economic unit—a household or a firm—is only a small part of the whole process of the social economy. "Each individual of the multitude of managers of firms and heads of households has to live together with the others in an exchange economy and in all his plans has to take account of the actions of other individuals and of *their* plans." [126] Therefore his daily, annual, etc., plan is "incomplete," it can only be a "partial" plan.

Even if we do not consider historical examples of these two basic systems in their pure, ideal form the significant aspect of Eucken's analysis is that we see their elements present not only in certain countries at certain times, but everywhere, at all times. For instance, the exchange of consumers' goods was curtailed in Sparta by serving meals in common in a community, and it is equally limited in contemporary totalitarian states by similar measures. Economic dependence still exists in China, where the professions of family members depend upon the will of the head of the family, as a central authority. An infinite number of examples taken from every living society could be given to show the presence of partial realizations of these two types of economic systems.

It is clear from this brief survey that each of these two ideal types of economic systems is strictly connected with the special distribution of powers, administrative systems, etc. Since, as the author emphasizes, each particular period contains these two systems in various configurations of their elements, this basic conception opens an avenue of approach towards a concrete, structural study of particular economic styles as expressed in various forms of powers, administration, etc.

But these two types of economy remain in mutual dependence upon two basic forms of markets, in terms of basic forms of supply and demand. Moreover, they are necessarily connected with main forms of possible monetary economy and the types of monetary systems.

Thus Eucken's conception of two basic economic systems as a ramified structure embracing all essential economic factors offers the solution to the Great Antinomy of economic studies. First, the necessary interrelations among various economic factors establish permanent and universally valid structures of economic reality. Already the form of an individual economic plan is significant, as we have seen, for all other factors. Second, the two economic systems enter into every scheme of economic life, not in pure, ideal form, but in elemental parts. On the basis of the previously established necessary connections between individual elements, from the change of one of them we can follow the possible consequent changes occurring in other factors. Thereby we can obtain access, through ideal, invariant structures, to the analysis of the changes occurring in the economic process, and of this process itself.

Eucken's theory claims to be a morphological system of pure economic types. As F. W. Meyer, quoted by Eucken, expresses it: "A morphological system is equivalent to an alphabet of individual letters, combinations of which can without great difficulty be made as needed for concrete problems," while "to construct theories for every possible combination of conditions would be a gigantic utopian enterprise like printing a book with a special alphabet for every different word." [127]

This morphology is matched by a corresponding economic theory. "As we have repeatedly shown in this book, because economic events make up an interdependent whole, economics itself must form an interconnected body of knowledge. . . . The structure and interrelationships of events and the way they all fit together, has to be matched by the interrelationships in the system of our scientific knowledge." [128] This theory ought to be developed on the basis of the morphological scheme. Created out of the observation of the real economic world morphology and theory are expected "to be tools for obtaining scientific experience" and "for achieving a scientific and penetrating understanding of economic phenomena. In this way they solve what is the central problem of a science, to reveal necessary relationships and unity where the naïve thinker sees only chance and arbitrariness." [129]

6. *The lived-world and the sciences of rational behavior*

To close our survey of methods and approaches in contemporary European social sciences, we will turn again to Husserl.

As Albert Salomon points out in his article, "German Sociology," it was predominantly Alfred Schütz who adapted Husserl's phenomenology in its most original and complete sense.[130] Schütz's method in social science relies not only upon the phenomenological method, as already presented, but also draws upon the developments in Husserl's philosophy which came after the *Logical Investigations* and *Ideas I*.[131]

After positing the methodological foundation of an apodictic inquiry into the nature of the universe as it is presented in the contents of consciousness, Husserl turns his attention in the *Cartesian Meditations* to a clarification of how the very nature of consciousness is instrumental in specific phenomena in which the universe appears to us. In other words, it is from the point of view of the constitutive activities of consciousness itself that the nature of the universe should be explained. At this point the already vast scope of the investigation is amplified by a new dimension. What is at stake is not merely the universe of things and beings, nature and social institutions, as we face them in our actual awareness of them. As Schütz himself stresses, Husserl's contribution to the foundation of social science is that each science—whether of nature or of culture—consists of systems of meanings instituted by the scientist.[132] Therefore scientific notions and concepts are rooted in the pre-theoretical *lived-world* (*Lebenswelt*), as the lived-world of the scientist and his fellow men, out of which they arise in connection with life and its deepest concerns. In order to be meaningful for this world, science should retain, even in its most advanced stages of development, contact with its initial source—the lived-world. It should keep the awareness of this significant nexus by constantly clarifying the relationship of the newly constructed notions to their initial source; the process of idealization and formalization, which the nature of the scientific procedure entails, tends toward separation and makes this difficult.

However, as Husserl shows in his last work (in which contemporary European science and culture are dealt with), it may happen, as with the positive sciences, that the ideal constructs of science itself are naïvely taken for lived-realities and substituted for the authentic lived-world. The aim of the constitutive analysis of consciousness is precisely to retrace the history of the constitutive mind and to disentangle the various complexes of meanings by which science, as well as current knowledge, has interpreted the original lived-world. Following retroactively all the steps of the successive sedimentations of meanings, constitutive phenomenology attempts to find again the way to the original experience out of which our lived-world arose, confronting the

interpretations with primary facts.[133] In this process of clarification of meanings the sclerotized strata of meanings become revitalized and so too does the world we live in. In this
sense the aim of phenomenology is a reconstitution of our
essentially human, authentic, lived-world. This genesis of the
world in our consciousness—which as the only constitutive
point of world reference is called "transcendental"—should
not be followed naïvely, within the *natural attitude*.[134] On
the contrary, since the constitutive consciousness is the phenomenologically "reduced" consciousness, the world in its
successive constitutive stages will appear in its universal,
invariant structures and laws. And in order to understand
the nexus between the constituents of Husserl's ample conception of phenomenology, taken as a philosophical system
rather than method alone, as a foundation of social science,
we should mention a third idea, which is complementary
and most fundamental. It deals with the rôle and conception of Time. As a matter of fact, the genesis of the lived-
world is simultaneously the genesis of consciousness; it proceeds in Time—Time, as understood by Husserl, and similar to Bergson's concept—is a *lived duration* of consciousness itself.[135]

Constitutive phenomenology can offer a foundation for the
concrete sciences investigating phenomena of the social world,
because in the first place, as Schütz says, all of them are fundamentally related to this primordial sphere of our lived-
world. In the second place, this private world emerging from
the activity of the individual and subjective consciousness
is already not only mine, but—as developed by Husserl in
the fifth and sixth *Cartesian Meditation*—also the world of
an *alter ego*, the Other, who appears in this world as a
psycho-corporeal element.[136]

The appearance of the Other in my subjective field of
constitutive consciousness makes my lived-world an intersubjective world of culture. As formulated by Schütz: "It is

intersubjective because we live in it as men among other men, bound to them through common influences and work, understanding others and being an object of understanding for others. It is a world of culture because, from the outset, the lived-world is a universe of significations to us, i.e., a framework of meaning (*Sinnzusammenhang*) which we have to interpret, and of interrelations of meaning which we institute only through our action in this lived-world." [137] Our common life with others in all its aspects not only takes place in our lived-world but is its essential constituent. Therefore, all forms of the social world can and should be investigated within the framework of the constitutive investigation of the lived-world. The social world refers constitutively to specifically "social" forms of subjective activity: *behavior* and *action*. Schütz's distinction between behavior and action becomes the key to his foundation for sciences of rational behavior.[138] The starting point is the stream of constitutive consciousness. Behavior (*Verhalten*) is characterized as *active* experience which spontaneously comes into being and passes out of being in the onflow of continuous duration without having a content of meaning. We understand *passive* experiences to be acts of reflection or recognition which ascribe meaning to other past or future experiences, and, as such complexes of meanings they remain in the consciousness. However, active experiences, as soon as they pass away, may be reflected upon and in this manner acquire meaning. They can be reflected upon also in anticipation of their occurrence in the future. If in this case, says Schütz, an act of intending joins that of reflection, we construct a project of future behavior. Action is defined as behavior according to some plan of such projected behavior. Thus, in contradistinction to behavior itself and other experiences, action is characterized by its meaningfulness. With respect to the types of their meaningfulness, Schütz distinguishes between *in-order-to motive* and *because motive* actions. The first signifies the purposefulness of an action and refers to the future; for instance, the project of going to a concert is my *in-order-to* motive for my driving to San Francisco. Its *because* motive may be that some soloist, whom I would particularly like to hear, is taking part in the performance. The *because* motive expresses concern with the reason or cause of an action, and refers to the past.

Understanding other people—the main problem of the social world—occurs on the basis of identifying other people's experiences with our own and from our interpretation of *in-order-to* and *because* motives of other people's actions in terms of the content of their consciousness. It is not the intent of such human understanding to influence the other person. The *in-order-to motives* in general do not intend to influence others. They constitute the first type of social action. The second type of social action occurs when the *in-order-to motive* is employed to change the Others' stream of consciousness—to influence them.

According to the intimacy and remoteness of our reach of the Other in our *in-order-to motive* actions—corresponding to the concreteness and abstractness of our experiences —Schütz distinguishes four layers of the social world. As he expresses it: "My social world with the *alter egos* in it is arranged, around me as the center, into associates, contemporaries, predecessors and successors, whereby I and my different attitudes to others institute these manifold relationships." [139]

The lived-world is, according to Schütz's analysis, also arranged into fields (*Zentren*); with respect "to my current state of interest, each one of them has its own peculiar center of density and fullness, and its open but interpretable horizons." [140] In connection with them, Schütz introduces two categories: *familiarity* and *strangeness*. It is a third category, namely, *accessibility*, at which the grouping of my environment is aimed. My environment is grouped into: (1) that which is actually within my direct, sensory reach; (2) that which is potentially accessible; and (3) that which, as only "attainable," lies before me as "an open horizon."

This basic model of the social world, in terms of the meaningfulness of human actions interpreted through subjective experiences, offers a contribution to the methodology and foundation of social sciences, in particular the sciences of rational behavior. As a result of the distinction between behavior and action, the succession of stages of behavior, understood currently in hypothetically constructed terms limited to the physical expression of behavior, can be explored at a meaningful level within the framework of Schütz's lived-world conception. As Schütz defines it: "Rational action is given when all the ends of action and all the means which will lead to it are clearly and distinctly presented, as, for example, in the case of economic action." [141] Because of the clarification of the nature of action as specified by its intelligible project, which in turn points back to the stream of experience in which our lived-world is constituted, the study of behavior is endowed not only with a fragmentary meaningfulness for single actions taken in isolation, but extends the scheme of meaningfulness of single actions to the all-embracing network of the lived-world, of which they are significant constituents.

Science itself operates with, and constructs "objective complexes of meanings" which correspond only approximately to the circumstances of the real world. If these objective complexes of meanings are "correct" they are "about subjective complexes of meanings" concerning some anonymous contemporaries of the scientist and his time.[142] However, the fact that the scientist's formalized theory can only approximate actual cases concerning living people does not rule out the legitimacy of his procedure, operating as it necessarily does with "ideal" types and not concrete individuals. The task of the methodology and foundation of social science for Schütz is, therefore, precisely to explain these objective complexes of meanings through the clarification of their relation to the subjective experience as universalized in the lived-world. According to Albert Salomon this point is the main feature of Schütz's original contribution to the methodology of social sciences.

3. Interpretation of results: the dynamic nature of man and the social universe.

Throughout the history of philosophy, society, social institutions, and the state have either applied basic philosophical theories, or have been conceived as their consequences. The concepts of society and its laws, standards, and aims have been intimately connected with the concept of man ever since Plato's *Republic*. Both in the notion of the primitive or "natural" state arising to facilitate man's survival, and in the theory of the "ideal" state which is oriented in all its pursuits to the aim of man's ultimate perfection, Plato is indeed referring to the crucial concept of man. In contemporary thought the traditional concept of man's nature has been put on trial; evidence brought from many sides sets philosophy the task of redefinition, necessitating an equally crucial change in the concept of society.

The concept of man which has prevailed in Western thought since Aristotle (expressed by his definition of man as "a rational animal capable of laughter"), and which has been interpreted within the framework of Aristotelian logic and metaphysics, has presented man statically. According to this concept, man is but one entity among others, and his essential nature seems to be a permanent set of properties which unambiguously demarcates him from other entities.

Although it was necessary to acknowledge man's physical mutability, this traditional concept did not go beyond the idea of a certain set of organic properties which, together with the faculty of reason, provided an appropriate basis for a wholly rational grasp of human "nature."

The crucial change which led to the new concept of man in contemporary phenomenological thought stems from the novel emphasis placed on the dynamic, ever-changing nature of man. In the light of new insights into man's development, pursuits, etc., the traditional Aristotelian set of properties would appear to be inadequate for the comprehension of human nature. For if man is in the process of becoming, no set of static properties can constitute his nature, nor can he be regarded as a self-centered isolated entity, an Aristotelian "essence," since he must be viewed as essentially related to others.

But in what, then, does human nature consist, if it is perpetually in the making? What is "the other man" for us? Is human nature to be identified with physical processes? Is "the other man" an object of Christian reverence, as in the mystical approach, or simply, at the other extreme, a co-existing organism? The phenomenologically oriented inquiries in psychology, psychopathology, and the social sciences, presented in this chapter, have suggested a stand on these questions which may be summarized as follows:

1. Man, unlike merely organic beings which are entirely products of nature, is essentially a *self-creative* being, who chooses his forms in full awareness and has aims transcending merely natural purposes.

2. The fundamental point of reference for man's self-creativity is the other man.

3. The social universe embracing every individual is nothing other than the resultant of a vast net of individual relations: a form of society is an extrapolation from the fundamental forms of tension in man's creative nature.

The scientific investigations above are well worth further scrutiny for the light they shed on these three points.

Concerning the first point, we have seen how the psychological researches of Jaspers, Binswanger, and their followers suggest the view that man cannot be conceived as confined to organic functions variously manifested. They strongly emphasize that, on the contrary, psychological and especially psychopathological inquiries demonstrate the existence and the role of a spiritual "existential" process in which man is basically involved, and which parallels the organic process. They recognize the purely metaphysical dimension toward which this spiritual process points. It might appear that there is nothing novel in stressing the spiritual side of man, for in various cultural trends throughout history the spiritual has not only been acknowledged, but even exaggerated to the point of denying the value of the organic. However, the phenomenological and existential approach to the role and nature of man's spiritual involvement is sharply distinguished from others in that it does not emphasize man's essentially spiritual nature to the point of making it at variance with the organic, as, for example with romanticism or the more recent views of German expressionism. In both of these trends, if the spiritual plays a crucial role, it is at the expense of the organic, natural part of man, and a perpetual strife between man's natural and spiritual tendencies is assumed. Man is depicted as caught in a tragic dilemma: he cannot fail to live a natural life which hinders intense spiritual activity. If he pursues his higher spiritual vocation, the overdevelopment of his spiritual faculties is assumed to destroy the body, and has been held responsible for the early death of many romantic poets and artists. Man appears committed to an irresolvable conflict which is the result of his incarnation, and from which only death can free him.

The existential approach offers a diametrically opposed interpretation of the relationship of man's natural and spiritual involvement. Among the three levels of this involvement, the natural, the spiritual or existential, and the purely metaphysical, neither a destructive strife nor a relationship in which one is privileged is assumed. On the contrary, the basic *tension* which relates each to the others expresses the basic truth that none of them can be conceived alone, but that each is the constructive condition for the other two.

Psychological investigation has shown that, at the lowest level of development, the human animal becomes "man" because even while securing himself organic survival, he also reaches beyond his vital needs in an effort which is no longer an egocentrically aimed expression of organic functions, but which transcends the narrow sphere of organic interests. Indeed, it appears that at no stage of his development can man be adequately grasped in his entirety, frozen in that stage, for he is essentially in process. None of his organic, vital, or mental concerns is intrinsically complete, but is related to the particular stage in which it occurs. None of these stages is a goal in itself that could express anything final in man; all of them aim higher in the constant tension which is man's most characteristic feature. It is the continuity of this pervasive tension among the three dimensions in which man is engaged that establishes their indispensable complementarity. Tension which comes from the organic depth, and tends to transcend nature, is continued in man's effort toward spiritual self-realization. It does not rest even there, but continues and culminates in the effort to transcend the narrow frame of his psyche in an all-encompassing *Transcendence*. At the level of his self-realization, man is engaged in a process of mastering the self, which combines the continuity of natural tension with the functions of reason in the recognition of forms, in analysis, and in choice. Thus man cannot be fully defined either as a product of nature, or as a product of nature endowed with reason. He is man, of course, insofar as he is both, but not in the sense that his organic and rational functions can be divided by any static borderline. Man appears as a dynamic being whose specific nature emerges as the resultant of the tensions which constitute the drive toward self-realization and offer freedom as a possible escape from the narrow limits of nature and mind.

In the cognition of man in this dynamic perspective where no static essence is available, a new criterion of adequacy has to be adopted. Intuitive knowledge of our own inner progress as well as of others adopts for its touchstone the most genuine goals which the individual alone honestly sets for himself. Measured in his actual progress with reference to these aims, man's realization, attitudes, actions, etc., are considered as "authentic," i.e., directly corresponding to those aims which involve an entire world view, or "inauthentic."

Psychological inquiry has shown not only that there is no opposition between the natural and the spiritual dimensions of man, but also that man's normal physical functioning and mental sanity require their co-ordination.

With reference to the second of the philosophical results summarizing our inquiry into the sciences, it has been brought into vivid focus that the dynamic nature of man does not isolate him either from the world or from his fellows. On the contrary, man is basically oriented toward the other man in *all* his functions. From the primitive functions necessary for survival to the highest functions of spiritual self-realization, man takes into account his community with others.

Economic inquiry has shown that basic individual economic plans refer to the more general plans of the community and society. We have already seen, from the anthropological investigations of Lévi-Strauss discussed in the preceding chapter, that the basis for the most primitive social relations is man's fundamental propensity to exchange goods. Various types of social relations underlying social institutions, such as justice, are rooted in individual conscious acts which, even at the most fundamental level, can be recognized as directed from one man to another, as social acts. Thus law, for instance, emerges as rooted in the basically social acts of man, not as a concept reducible to the evolutionary stages of civilization. Even at the lowest level where we can differentiate the functions of man in his effort to emerge into the lived-world, the very rationality of his acts and actions lies in their being outer-directed. Thus man has been considered not only a self-creative being, but simultaneously a *socio-creative* being.

Finally, with reference to the third point above, the formation of social groups of many sorts (as basic as the family, the cornerstone of some types of society), has occurred as a result of man's basic orientation toward the other man at the higher spiritual level of love. The perpetuation of these social groups, in the perspective of traditions and posterity owes as much to man's creative activity as he owes the other man in shaping himself. Inquiry into all levels of man's socio-creative being reveals that social institutions are not externally imposed, but are expressions of the deepest nature of the individual. Nor is it necessary, it appears, for man to oppose the prevalent social forms in order to defend his rights for a chosen type of realization, for the form of society takes its very meaning from the types of human relations from which it arose and, ultimately, from the types of individual human realizations. Therefore it is not legitimate either externally to impose a social form for any purpose, or to make the social form an end in itself. The form of society is the extension of the forms of man's basic tensions, expressed by their interrelations within a universe which is at once the result of these interrelations and the milieu in which man may strive to attain his own self-realization.

THREE : *The World*

1. Man and nature in Heidegger's intentional conception of the world.

We have seen in our preceding discussion how man has been saved from being completely included in nature; in some aspects he is part of nature, in others he is distinct. Yet the question of the relation between man and nature has remained open. Dominating the entire course of modern philosophy is the idea that man is caught in a perpetual strife with Nature, struggling to sustain himself in the midst of her overwhelming powers. This conflict, this dualism, is usually attributed to the Cartesian formulation of the essentially human in terms of consciousness, as contrasted with nonconscious extended bodies. However, the concepts of uniqueness of man's mind and the "true reality" to which they are supposed to give access, both implying a depreciation of the natural realm, go back not only further than Descartes, but even further than Plato: they are already pres-

ent in outline in Parmenides. In order to find a view of the
world in which man and nature are conceived within one
homogeneous system, it is necessary to go back as far as the
pre-Socratics; the pre-Socratics did not differentiate the universe into heterogeneous realms but sought a single principle
with reference to which all aspects of the universe could be
explained. Subsequent interpretations of these first attempts
of Thales, Anaximander, and Anaximenes to grasp the principles of unity and diversity in the universe distorted their
intentions by putting undue emphasis on the organic or
physical nature of the principles proposed.

In fundamental contrast, modern philosophy stemming
from Descartes took as its basic reference point the immaterial consciousness and led to Kant's extreme view of the
transcendental consciousness by reference to which the status
of nature is depreciated. Consciousness was conceived of as
an autonomous cognitive agency, creative of the universe of
knowledge, which follows its own rules. These rules become
laws of the universe-as-we-know-it. But Kant himself emphasized that this consciousness, although creating all knowledge, is, with respect to nature as it is "in itself," like a tiny
island in an immense and unchartable sea. Thus the opposition of the mind and the organic is not overcome; between
them remains an abyss, now formulated as the opposition
between the knowable and the utterly unknowable.

Within the phenomenologically oriented current of ideas
the first and most systematic doctrine of the relation between
nature and man has been advanced by Martin Heidegger.
In the framework of his theory of the world these two traditionally divorced dimensions find the possibility of recon-
ciliation. The shift from the search for a middle ground
which can link the opposed factions to the search for a third
level at which both of them are primordial, has become the
groundwork for all further treatment of the issue.

Heidegger's thought parallels that of the pre-Socratics insofar as he takes a point of departure in which dualism is absorbed into a single system which can explicate both man and nature. However, insofar as Husserl's doctrine of the intentionality of consciousness is adopted, he is drawing upon the modern heritage which culminates in Husserl's theory of the *absolute* status of intentional consciousness.

A crucial question arises in Heidegger's thought: How can the intentionality of consciousness be a basic condition for both man and nature without prejudicing their relationship, without resulting in a subjectivistic conclusion? Although Heidegger's main problem, the meaning of being, can be seen in embryo in Husserl's *Ideas*, he tries from the very start to avoid the idealistic conclusion which was reached in this work as a result of the emphasis placed upon consciousness. (This conclusion Husserl attempted to avoid in all his later work.) Heidegger assumes that the intentionality of consciousness is prior to man's emergence as an understanding being and to the emergence of the world-for-man as a system of meanings. Thus intentionality is the key factor which together with nature underlies the essentially human world. Thus the essentially human does not consist merely in some faculties distinguishing man from the rest of the universe but, on the contrary, *includes* him in the world which is man's necessary counterpart.

The schema of the investigation is determined by the emphasis Heidegger places on the creativity of the intentional consciousness. In the Kantian approach consciousness had also been adduced as the creative point of reference for the knowable world. However, in opposition to the Kantian conception, Heidegger, in joining man's creative prerogative to the powers that condition man, is not conceiving intentional consciousness in terms of a set of static rules and laws fixed once and for always for a recurring universe. He assumes at the start that man is involved within a perpetual self-creative process with respect to the world. In other words, consciousness is not construed merely as creating an external world which recurs, but as constantly re-creating the individual man with reference to the world which emerges through the same operations.

To reconstruct in this dynamic perspective the balance between man and nature entails a challenge to the traditional categories in which the world has been described. In particular, the concepts of physical object, space, and time, which since the earliest philosophy, as well as in common sense, have been taken as the world's skeleton, are formulated in a radically different way.

The world is one of the essential themes of Martin Heidegger's ontology and his conception of it represents his masterpiece. Heidegger gives to the world problem a new ontological formulation which avoids the presuppositions underlying the current traditional conception of the world in philosophy and science, and he attempts a basic reorientation of this conception.

In his inaugural lecture in 1930,[143] Heidegger's starting point is the statement that the fields of the particular sciences lie far apart. Their methods are fundamentally different. The roots they once had in a common ground are actually atrophied. Nevertheless, in each science—following its most specific intention—we are related to *what there is*. Precisely from the point of view of the science, no field precedes another in importance; nature does not precede history nor history nature. It is the world relationship which runs through all the sciences as such that constrains them to seek for *what there is* as an object of investigation, intending to present it in its *quiddity* and in its particular modality. What science accomplishes, whatever the momentary approach of the scientist may be, is an approximation of the essential nature of all things. The possibility and the nature of science, as well as the role of the scientist responsible for science, can be understood only from the point of view of the world relationships themselves.

Is this world relationship, however, to be understood in the sense of the Aristotelian ontology, or in the contemporary physicalistic sense?

Heidegger places himself at the point where science as a human activity arises. Man—one entity among others—"pursues" science; this means an irruption of a particular entity, called "man," into the whole of *what there is;* and in such a way that, in and through this irruption, *what there is* presents itself in its nature in the form of knowledge. From this particular position which man occupies with respect to the totality of what is, Heidegger approaches the world as a *human world*. Science is seen as a human activity based upon the inseparability of man and the world from one another. We should not, however, immediately jump to the conclusion that this means that Heidegger relates science and the world to man's subjectivity. On the contrary, proceeding beyond contemporary scientific theories about the animal "world," his basic assumption is that of the intersubjective, communicable and intelligible character of the human world, which means neither a purely idealistic "imprisonment," nor only the "brute reality" of the physicalistically understood nature.

As far as this latter approach is concerned, the overwhelming necessity of overcoming the conception of the world's "objectivity"—understood as Cartesian *res extensa*—was already felt in biology as early as the beginning of the century. In his *Theoretical Biology* Von Uexküll distinguishes three different strata of animal functions: the *world as sensed (Merkwelt)*,[144] the *inner world (Innenwelt)*,[145] and the *world of action (Wirkwelt)*. There is a periodic circulation between them, which Uexküll calls the *function-circle*. Von Uexküll insists that it is impossible to describe the biology of an animal otherwise than by an inquiry into his *function-circle*. Within the individual *function-circle*, the animal and his milieu constitute a unity comparable to a texture, which is achieved by the "constructive projection" or "plan" (*Bauplan*) of the animal, which in turn determines its observation and action (*Merkplan* or *Wirkplan*). Consequently, Von Uexküll is led to admit as many "worlds" or, better, "environments" as there are animals. As a matter of fact, following Von Uexküll's example, if we consider the sea animals only superficially, we may think that they live in a common and uniform "world" (or "environment"). On closer examination it appears, however, that different types of sea animals possess different forms of life and accordingly different specific "environments," which are reciprocal cause and effect relationship with the individual constructive projection of each animal.[146] If we consider the "world" as temporal and spatial, there is, according to Von Uexküll, no *one* and the same space and time, but there are *as many* various spaces and times *as there are* animals (subjects) within their environments, "since each of them possesses its own space and time, namely, the space and time determined by the individual's functional circle."

Von Uexküll concludes that to admit only a unique world (which for man is called "reality")—understood as adequately similar to our own environment and this latter extended (enlarged) in all directions in time and space—is nothing but a convenience of thought. Drawing a parallel between animal and man, he affirms that in order to understand man's actions we have to consider them from the point of view of his particular situation (*Spezialbühne*). However, when a man attempts to describe the "worlds" of his friends and to show how they behave in the world as *human beings,* the conception of the "world" as an "environment" formed for the animals manifests itself as insufficient. The animal's environment, determined by his particular functional system, is understood as an *island of senses (Sinnesinsel)*.[147] These various "worlds" could be considered, therefore, as purely "subjective," since they are determined by the individual animal and for his sake only as a system of various opportunities for the development of the senses, closed within the circumference of his functional system, and untransferable.

Therefore, such a conception of the world appears too narrow for human beings since man, in opposition to the animals, has not only an individual and social but also a common "objective" world—the world of thought. On the other hand, man's individual world, extending into his intersubjective world of thought, is not determined by nature, as is that of the animal. Consider an oak tree (example taken from Binswanger)[148] from the point of view of the role it plays in the "world" of an owl that dwells in the oak's empty trunk, in that of a songbird that has its nest in the oak's high branches, in the environment of a fox in its hole under the oak's roots, in that of a bird seeking a grub in the wood of the oak, and in that of this grub itself. If we now consider further the role the same oak plays in the world of a hunter, a calculating wood merchant and a romantically inclined girl, we cannot, according to Uexküll, fail to see the difference. While an animal is bound to his constructive project and cannot overcome it, a human being also has the possibility of being a hunter, of selling wood, or of being pensive, besides an infinite number of other possibilities. Furthermore, such a possibility of a different "world projection" is strictly connected with a different self-projection. The human self is different if a man is a hunter, projecting a hunter's world; a dreaming girl; or a calculating wood merchant. And insofar as the self-projection differs, so does the world projection.

A strict polarity of man and his world as interchangeable insofar as their particular character is concerned—such a world projection corresponding to such a self-realization and vice versa—and self-realization conceived, as by Jaspers, as a matter of free decision and choice form Heidegger's essential approach, relating the world to man and man to the world as one indivisible, or rather inseparable, structure, thus overcoming the classical, Cartesian separation between *res cogitans* and *res extensa*.

Furthermore, what is conceived in classical thought as definable in terms of a static, everlasting *human nature*, appears in the light of the contemporary inquiry as a being in process. Not only trends of thought and sets of sensibility undergo cultural and social evolution. Even what previously was considered solid and unshakable—man's cognitive powers and the nature of his cognition itself—appears, in the light of later psychological and sociological inquiry, to be undergoing basic changes such as those concerning the nature of perception and of categories. Are we therefore forced to admit that there is no limit to this process, and consequently that there should be assumed a complete unpredictability as to what and how the world projections form themselves and *can* be formed?

The basis upon which Heidegger understands the unified structure of man and the world also provides an answer to this question. Heidegger escapes relativism by attempting to offer a fundamental explanation of man's world, valid as long as man remains man. What is the ultimate "nucleus" of "humanity" as opposed to "animality" or "thingness"? What characterizes man as man is that all his cognitive, volitional, and emotional acts will tend "towards . . . an object, an object of cognition, will, desire, love. . . ." Man does not perform actions automatically but is conscious of objects of his acts. This "intentional" character of man's consciousness, put forward by Brentano and adopted in a modified form by Husserl as fundamental to phenomenological inquiry, is extended by Heidegger from the subjectivity of consciousness into the objectivity of man's common world.

One can perhaps interpret Heidegger's world conception by affirming that whatever particular shapes man and his world may assume, it will always be in the framework of the essential modes of intentionality. The apparent "distance" between an individual *cogitans* and the world "around him" which led classical thinkers to consider them as radically different in nature—while in reality they might be both physical and intellectual—is the "distance" between an object of intention and its source. Man, understood as a source of intentions, as a pole of a basic structure of intentional relations, is called by Heidegger *Dasein*.[149] As such he has an ontological structure radically different from any other type of being or thing. He is not solid like things of nature, like, for example, a stone or a table. But his difference from an animal is also crucial. The milieu of an animal is determined by nature; the animal has neither independence nor freedom to change it; he is forever in his specific situation.

Man, for Heidegger as for Jaspers, is also determined biologically by nature and therefore, like the animal, also has his milieu. But beyond this he has possibility, freedom to give a form to his self, to his life, according to his choice. In Heidegger's own terms "it belongs to man's specific mode of being to be concerned with his being, since it is up to him to decide about himself and he may gain or lose so far as his being is concerned." [150] Man's permanent *instability* consists in this essential freedom, distinguishing him from the solidity of thingness. Man's concern with the possibilities about which he himself must decide gives to him his most specific character. Effectively it is man's capacity to be *concerned with*[151] which constitutes the most fundamental aspect of intentionality. The extension of man's cognition, desires, feelings—intentions—delimits man's universe. They are the basis of each world project, relating it to the particular individual. However, the basis for such a structure, unifying such various, different and also often contradictory intentions, is the fact that man's intentions lead toward the object of his *concern;* they reach as far as his *concern* reaches. Whatever the form of concern may be (whether it is the curiosity of an explorer, an emotional interest, or the vital interest to protect one's life) and whatever the object, the reach of man's concern prescribes his world. "The impact of everyday needs of the adversities of life, of our effort to provide and entertain our everyday existence," says Heidegger, "are possible only because *Dasein* is in its very nature oriented by our concern." [152] Here, however, an important question is to be examined. We have contrasted the *human world* to that of the animal's environment in virtue of the fact that the latter is entirely referred to one subject, is "subjective," while the former is infra-human, common to all men, "objective." Nevertheless, the human world, conceived as the structure of man's concern, appears thereby limited for every particular individual to the domain of his concern: to a peasant the world is identical with his fields, to a merchant with his shop, etc. Therefore doubt arises about the infra-subjective community of such worlds. In addition, Heidegger insists upon the fact that by no effort could the world as a whole be grasped without being vitiated by the particular perspective of its author, such a perspective being based upon his own experience with a particular section of things and beings. Are we here facing a new form of Kantian transcendental idealism? In answer to this question two points must be carefully distinguished:

1. In Heidegger's conception concern does not create its object. Both intentionality and the world are rooted in the fact that man, as an intentional being (*Dasein*), is what he is in his very nature in strict reference to something other than himself. The theories of man's imprisonment in his own individual being, are, in this perspective, inadequate, and hide the essential state of affairs: man would not be man if he did not, essentially and basically, refer to what is

apart from him; he can subsist only in a much larger net of relations within the totality of *what there is*. In the analysis which Heidegger offers of the fundamental structures of intentionality, man's fundamental reference to the world takes the form of a unitary structure of intentional relations, as *being-in-the-world*. The word *in* obviously does not mean here a spatial or material inherence, but man's strict and constructive reference to the world. The world itself, however, in the light of its intentional reference, is understood not as a sum of objects, or as matter, a "brute physical reality," but as a net of relations or rather a system of relations between man (*Dasein*) and the realities of his surroundings, as objects of his concern.

2. A second explanatory consideration concerning the apparently transcendental conception of the world as presented by Heidegger is offered by the above comparison with the animal's environment. The animal's environment refers to the functional circle of one individual. It remains within the limits of its structure which is participated in only by this individual and is untransmittable. Man's world is also encircled first by his biological determination. Then it is determined by the particular individual reference or by the concern of a particular individual, having its source in his individual intentional acts. This world is, by the very nature of these acts, rational, and therefore transmittable to every other individual. It thereby transcends the narrow form of individuality extending into a world commonly shared by humanity, the world of thought, science, the arts, etc.

The difficulty is nevertheless not yet completely overcome, since man, understood as a source of intentionality, is at the same time a man determined and, one might say, cut off from other individuals by his "selfhood," by his autonomy. Indeed, it is by referring to himself as an "I" that man (*Dasein*) explicitly manifests himself as *being-in-the-*

world.[153] Therefore the question of a "subject" also arises at this level of intentionality, since selfhood is connected in traditional terminology with substantiality and personality. By "subject," in the current philosophical understanding, is meant a closed, encapsulated, psychological subject, understood as delimited from other beings by being himself.

In Heidegger's thought, on the contrary, selfhood is considered first of all at the intentional level; it appears as an aspect of man's being, conceived as *concerned with*. Since man's being consists in his "being concerned with," [154] it is from this character of concern that he obtains his permanent selfhood. "The autonomy (of the self) does not mean a confinement in individual being *(Seinsabgrenzung)* but existentially means nothing other than a current disposition for making decisions *(Vorlaufende Entschlossenheit)*." [155] Selfhood belongs to the structure of man's concern. However, concern is not founded in selfhood. To the full structural content of concern (Heidegger talks about "existentiality" as the *constitutivum* of concern) belongs both the autonomy of selfhood and the alternative possibility of factual abolition into dependence *(Unselbstständigkeit)*. In this perspective the ontological nature of subjectivity, considered in a substantial form and embodied in personality, as aspects or foundations of the selfhood, should be considered not at the most basic level but already at the level of the more specific nature of man. In other words, the currently admitted self-limitation of a so-conceived subject would be formed at the level of a more specific structure, while the fundamental selfhood of man, understood at his primordial intentional level, does not cut him off by any barrier from the totality of world structures.

The final precision, however, of the intentional selfhood is possible only within the totality of the structures of concern, interpreted in the sense which, according to Heidegger, determines the entire *humanity* of man.

Here Heidegger's thought expects to reach its crucial achievement. From the unsharable, strictly individual, ground of "brute" physical functions the human being, considered in his world as an intelligible and rational being in an intelligible and rational world, achieves a unity between himself and the world of things and other beings. This unity at the same time solves the problems concerning the apparently radical difference between *res cogitans* and *res extensa* and the problems of solipsism, which, in the light of this conception, appear as *"Scheinprobleme,"* or at least as not fundamental problems. These problems are translated into terms of the specific level of structure without, however, reducing one to the other.

In fact, after having discarded the Cartesian conception of the world, Heidegger not only does justice to the importance of *extensio* as manifested in the world (Descartes), but also as related to man. Considered at the most fundamental level, that of intentionality, the realities of man's environment do not consist, indeed, in the "objective" view of things that surround us (by "objective" is meant "objectified by perception"). We know them, of course, as objects, but at the fundamental level of our concern with [156] them they are nothing more than utensils (*pragmata*). Everything which we can use, in the largest sense of the term, is a utensil; a knife, a book, a train, etc. A utensil is not identical with a thing—it does not exist independently. It exists only in the context of a double reference; that toward other utensils and that toward a man (*Dasein*). A needle demands both thread and a tailor to represent what it is; considered without thread and as essentially serving nobody, it is absurd. Each utensil refers to the whole system of utensils, and as each utensil contains a reference to a type of *Dasein,* the world appears as a system of systems of those referential relations. Man (*Dasein*) is the ultimate point of reference, which does not refer any further but exists in itself. However, he can exist only in this particular mode of being, within these referential relations. It is man who is the source of the possibilities which engender the system of relations and which, as a whole, constitute the world. These possibilities of man give meaning to things, posit them as an intelligible totality which we call "the world." Pragmata and man (*Dasein*) constitute together the *inner-world-beings,* that is, they are related spatially. Both man and pragmata are more or less "distant" from each other and "oriented" toward each other. However, the spatiality of the world as formed by the *inner-world-beings* is not that of three dimensions, quantitative and objectively measurable—this spatiality belongs to the "brute reality in the background." The distance under which man operates intentionally has no direct relation to "brute" physical distance: today we experience New York as being *closer* to Paris than Paris to Warsaw. Man (*Dasein*) is fundamentally oriented toward diminishing distances; for example, there are all kinds of increasing speeds in which we participate today, which aim at overcoming distance. Man has been immensely successful in bringing the world closer by radio and television and thus enlarging his everyday surroundings.

Pragmata are ordered spatially as being above or below, before or after, following each other, etc.; a neighbor's house is "five minutes' walk" away, school is "at a driving distance," etc. We see here that the world, for Heidegger, is spatial neither in the Cartesian nor in the Kantian sense; "space is neither in the subject, nor is the world in space." [157] The spatiality of the world, conceived as an intentional system, means the essential constitutive organization of man (conceived as a net of intentions and their source) toward other beings in the world totality. This does not mean the negation of the pure metric science of space (geometry). It simply means that the latter is a constitution posterior to that of intention and is irrelevant to the constitution of the *human* world, of the *human reality* which are here interchangeable notions. Insofar as man is conceived as related to the world, this world itself is man's world, is "humanized."

The spatiality of man, understood as a feature of intentionality, consists precisely in the fact that he "occupies space." Again, however, it is by no means in the sense of physical, metrical space but in the sense of "a field of action (*Spielraum*) within the circle of the nearest objects of his concern and their totality, this field being opened by man's concerned orientation and distance." [158] The extension of man and world in space is rooted, however, in an ultimate constitutive ground: temporality. Here Heidegger, following Husserl, seeks in temporality the ultimate source from which intentionality itself proceeds.[159] It is the fundamental mode of time that is in question when we ask what "renders possible the entire unified structure of man's concern in its multiple articulations (*Gliederungen*)." [160] In other words, referring to the general, essential character of man mentioned above, the question can be formulated as, "What makes it possible that man can be primarily concerned with his own being?" In point of fact the constitutive structure of man's concern—composed of four fundamental structures; those of recognition (*Verstehen*), feeling (*Befindlichkeit*), fall (*Verfallen*), and discourse (*Rede*) appear on a closer examination to be composed of forms or shapes which take time, which underlie the intentional projection. We can grasp the phenomenon of temporality in its three phases. On that of the future is based the fact that intention "projects" itself toward a possibility of man in view of what he is. The *revelation* (*Erschliessen*) to man of what he could be is found in the future as his possible realization. Therefore, the future is not founded on the present, since the man who does not actually make the decision to realize himself "temporizes," keeps at a distance and yet anticipates the

future out of which the real future proceeds. And it is a sort
of future extended in what we call "present time." The
present is understood as the phase of decision itself; therefore it is durationless, a bare moment. Neither of them is
static. Nor are they simply "dynamic," rather, they project
themselves *"ek*-statically." The phase of the past is that
which underlies those of our intentions which take the form
of moods. They represent an intention that, caught in its
natural projection, would like to return upon itself, cannot,
and "forgets itself." In order to be able to forget himself,
man needs to have *existed* before.

Primordial temporality, as understood by Heidegger, consists in phases of a dynamic projection of intentionality as
such. It is at the same time its dynamic nature since in
the nature of its phases lies the possibility of the various
forms and, so to speak, "incarnations" of intentionality in
different specific characters of the rich human constitution
being unified in one homogeneous underlying structure.
The very character of intentionality, its projecting itself toward its object, is comprised in the *"ek*-static" character of
temporality in all its three phases; future, present and past,
and their dynamic unity. In this sense temporality presents
the necessary condition for man existing as an intentional
being. In this way Heidegger attempts to grasp the entire
structure of man's "life" or, in other terms, of his complete
"functioning," man being specifically a dynamic (non-static,
but *ek*-static) being. But by the same stroke, by the fact
that man is rooted in temporality, his *being-in-the-world*
and the world itself are explained: for man to be situated
among other beings he must find himself in a world. This
latter, in its turn, shapes itself in reference to man. Man
projects himself by the force of temporality. "As long as man
proceeds in time, so long is there a world," Heidegger
sums up, and "If no man were to exist, there would then

be no world." [161] Temporality as currently understood would be a specific form, derived from this fundamental one.

Thus temporality is so strictly connected with the structure of the world, its own structure is so reflected in the latter, that the specific structures of the world are founded in temporal structures, and these take the shape of spatial relations, all together reflecting—as a world projection—the human individual projecting them.

Here, however, the question of the subjectivity of the world comes up again. Heidegger formulates it in the following way: "If the subject is ontologically understood as an existing man (*Dasein*) whose being is rooted in temporality, then we should say: the world is subjective. However, this subjective world as *temporal and therefore transcendental* would be more objective than any possible object." [162]

2. Interworldly connections and the anthropological conception of man's being-in-the-world.

Phenomenologically oriented research constitutes the attempt to unify the disciplines which, through centuries, have become more and more fragmented. However, the basis for unification is no longer a speculative metaphysical one entailing a bifurcation of man and nature, nor is it a purely physical one submerging man in nature. The basis is a concrete analytic ground where philosophical analysis and scientific inquiry meet in an "anthropological" investigation of man regarded both as emerging from nature and as transforming nature into *his* world. This anthropological inquiry is characterized by an empirical approach while yet acknowledging the supernatural dimension of man.

Descartes' ontological distinction of the two substances, mind and body, which until the most recent times underlay the formulation of philosophical and scientific problems in terms of the subject-object opposition, was not only the reason of the whole complex of problems in philosophy centered around the controversy about the existence of the external world, but its impact also was reflected in science. Sciences such as psychology, psychiatry, medicine, which have to deal with both sides of the opposition, were searching for a simultaneous key to both of them. In fact, the main effort in these fields could be interpreted as directed toward finding a bridge between mind and body, apparently so disparate and still somehow connected. Innumerable such attempts could be quoted, from occasionalism to psycho-physiological parallelism.

At the beginning of this century, however, the attitude of philosophers and researchers changed. Instead of looking for an explanation of the union of two heterogeneous elements, they tried to formulate problems of mind and body without the assumption of such heterogeneity. On one side, behavioristic psychology, developed and ramified into behavioral sciences of sociology, economics, etc., and the psychology of form, and, on the other side, Heidegger's philosophy found a large audience among both philosophers and natural scientists.

Behavioral science is overcoming the mind-body division by transposing the inquiry into a "neutral" level, viewing comportment as expressing the total human being. In its philosophical interpretation of behavior and the mind-body problem itself, however, it considers itself to have overcome the problem by reducing all phenomena to *bodily*, physical phenomena, thus dispensing entirely with the second alternative, mind.

Heidegger's position is different at this point. He attempts to overcome the separation between mind and body, subject and object, "external" and "immanent" by considering both parts of the alternative—mind and the so-called "external world"—at the level of their most fundamental structure where all heterogeneity between them is abolished, and they are, on the contrary, constituted, so to speak, *simultaneously*, one with reference to the other. At this level, where the essential nature of man is understood as *being-in-the-world*, the problem of the man-world relationship is shifted from that of a relation between two composite parts to the question of how man and the world constitute themselves in a reciprocal simultaneity. As a matter of fact, the phenomenological trend in psychology, psychiatry and psychopathology has found in the conception of man as a being, not opposed to, but comprised *within* the world and its time-space structure, a source of fundamental anthropological insights leading to a readjustment of methods. The psychologists and psychiatrists are turning their attention to the study of man as an intentional being—in an "anthropological" sense as an empirical inquiry—in the fundamental temporal and spatial structure of his world-projection. Binswanger calls this specific kind of inquiry a *"Daseins analytische"* anthropology. In this context we can only mention the essential aims of this inquiry, which is being pursued in various fields by a large number of researchers and practitioners.[163]

First of all, from the conception of man as comprised within but at the same time as projecting his world, the conclusion is drawn that for man nothing can be experienced outside his particular world-projection. This amounts (in a sense) to a Kantian interpretation of the structure of *being-in-the-world*, as a condition of possibility of experience as such ("natural" experience). Mental diseases, for whose symptoms explanation is required, can be phenomenologically analyzed as particular forms of experiences. The Heideggerian conception of the time-space structure of the world as a *matrix* of basic forms of experiences can therefore be considered as a *norm,* or to use a now current expression, as a basic *model* of inquiry. In this perspective mental disease does not cease to be related to its functional organic conditions; but it consists and manifests itself in the spatial world-projections of the patient. The inquiry into disease consists in describing the patient's world-projection and in comparing its deviations with the norm. The abnormality is expressible in terms of deviations from the model insofar as the time and space structure, and the texture, materiality and dynamism expressing them, are concerned.[164] Anthropological research offers both the fundamental diagnosis of the disease for clinical purposes and the fundamental explanation of terms such as *fear, phobia,* etc., in terms of the particular structure of a world projection.[165] The anthropological approach meets other methods of phenomenological psychology, which although referring rather to Bergson than to Heidegger as an initial source of inspiration, have developed a similar framework of inquiry. Almost all fields of psychology, pathological and normal, as for example characterology, emotivity, moods, etc., operate with the basic concepts of world-projection and spatio-temporal norms.

Just as the world-projection of an individual is considered as the basis of textures of character,[166] for instance his "avarice," so are the moods in their manifestations. What in poetic language is expressed as "elevating," "uplifting," or "debasing," indicating a direction in the "dynamic movement" of moods (often stated in the Rorschach test), finds —as we will see—a full explanation in the analysis of the spatiality of the world-projection and of the individual creating it. This anthropological explanation clarifies the meaning of the fundamental metaphors of psychopathological experiences such as "height," "elevation," "depth," "degradation," "fall," etc.; it also offers clues for therapy. The anthropological inquiry into emotivity and moods started by Binswanger found an important elaboration in works of Gaston Bachelard and Robert Desoille, and became an indispensable tool in psychiatry.

1. *Methodological and clinical applications of the anthropological approach*

As an illustration of the contributions of the anthropological approach to psychopathological research and practice as well as to problems of foundation and methodology in general, we shall present the following case analyzed by Binswanger.[167]

A young girl at any reference to the splitting or detaching of a heel from a shoe showed psychological disturbance culminating in fainting. These abnormal symptoms were related to an incident in her early life. When she was about five years old, while skating, the heel of her shoe remained in her skate. Freudian psychoanalysis interprets this fear as originating in birth fantasies—birth meaning detachment from the mother. In order to explain, however, why this *particular individual* had developed the heel phobia, since, according to Freudian theory, everybody experiences birth trauma and some without developing a hysterical "detachment" phobia, the concept of disposition was required. It is precisely this concept which, anthropologically treated, can in Binswanger's view provide a full explanation of the case. According to a fundamental methodological assumption, the world projection of the patient, being still more fundamental than the birth fantasies, appears to be dominated here by the category of continuity. Everything which the patient conceives to be significant is bound within a net of strict and static continuous connections. This continuity alone renders the world secure for her. For this reason the detachment from the mother took on such an overvalued importance. Both the birth trauma, as the fixation point of the "disposition," and the manifestation of the latter in the fear of each splitting and detachment in the concrete world, are rooted in the particular shape of the patient's world projection. The narrowness of this latter means at the same time a corresponding, abnormal "diminishment" of the patient, preventing her from maturing. In her world projection everything should remain static in order to maintain the character of continuity. The world projection, which, as entirely static, provides no fundamental security, is fragmented by every change, resulting in the splitting of the established continuity. Consequently change is synonymous for her with irremediable breakdown and her experience of it results in fear or panic. What is called an anxiety attack (*Angstanfall*) in psychopathology would, in this perspective, refer to the specific modification of the temporality within the above-mentioned world projection. As a matter of fact, under the impact of the continuity category, "normal temporality" in its past and present phases oriented toward the third phase of the future is here considered as deformed and the predominant importance attributed to the past. In the patient's perspective the world should remain what it is. Therefore the temporal moment of suddenness, as characteristic of everything which breaks apart, splits and destroys the actual world, takes on an enormous importance and constitutes the basis of the patient's fear. In this outlook the general phenomenon of *phobia* means an attempt to confer security on an abnormally narrowed world projection.[168]

In general the vast amount of research being carried on by leading European phenomenologists in psychology and the related sciences permits one to consider Binswanger's view as generally valid. This conception of man in terms of his fundamental structure as *being-in-the-world* has offered to this branch of psychology a *norm*, a philosophical foundation, and a correspondingly reoriented method for inquiry into the human person.

2. *Spatio-temporal norms in psychological and psychiatric practice*

In his book *Time as Experienced*, Minkowski introduces the problem of space and time as the central problem of psychology. As a source of conflicts, this problem seems to him to pertain to the whole of contemporary culture. The laws of normal spatial and temporal structure established by Minkowski in his classic inquiry were inspired by Husserl's phenomenological studies of temporality and Bergson's conception of *élan vital*. They correspond to Heidegger's basic conception analyzed in the present chapter.[169]

Minkowski deliberately accepts Bergson's *élan vital* as the basic, dynamic source of the human being. The "self" can assert itself as a living personality only within the "vital impulse." To discover how it can do this, we must analyze the phenomenon: "I go onward and try to realize something." The actual realization of our aim, however, is a factor of only secondary importance, for even an action resulting in failure is an affirmation of the "self" as part of the general vital impulse. In other words, it is the attempt to achieve a result which creates life, not the achievement itself, which is important. This "personal impulse" is a primary element, and consequently cannot be divided for analytical purposes. This phenomenon could be described by a scheme in the form of a vector:

self————achievement
personal
impulse

But we must not overlook the spatial and temporal character of such a basic phenomenon. On the one hand, it directly points "toward . . ." like a vector, which is always directionally oriented. On the other hand, the "achievement" does not suddenly come out of the "impulse," but becomes gradually present in it. The self and the thing achieved are merged in the "becoming." It is this temporal aspect of the vital impulse that Minkowski wants first to emphasize. The vectoral character of the impulse, however, implies spatiality.

Furthermore, a significant distinction must be made between Bergson's vital impulse, the general flowing onward of all things, and the "personal impulse," which is our participation in that general instinct, linking ourselves and the goals we try to achieve. Since this vital impulse is considered by Minkowski as the real basis of human personality, the main question about the self is how the personal impulse can remain distinct from the general impulse. Here again the spatial aspect is most revealing: the emerging vital impulse could not subsist otherwise than by "surrounding" itself with a halo of irrational factors, which extend further and further, forming at a limit a personal "horizon." This extension is a condition of its subsistence. Though in some moments of our life we may have the impression that our personal impulse is of very little importance in the world, still we always keep on acting. This perseverance of self is made possible, according to Minkowski, only because our personal impulse includes a super-individual factor which is our real reason for being. This factor, on a spiritual level, is the feeling of being part of a more general moving onward, of accomplishing a mission. It constitutes a further spatial dimension, integrating the self into the world. To this "horizontal" dimension should be added, however, the "vertical" dimension of the *élan vital*, leading, as we will see later on, to what Freud calls the "abysmal psychology" of subconsciousness. Consequently, we can say that for Minkowski the essence of life is not "a feeling of being, of existence," but a feeling of participation in a flowing onward, necessarily expressed in terms of time, and secondarily in terms of space. Here we see how Minkowski's conception, although independently developed, joins that of Heidegger and of Heideggerians: both are expressed in forms of time and space, and the disorders in the basic psychological life of a mental patient will signify modifications and weakenings of the vital impulse, expressed in modifications of their spatio-temporal structures. It is, however, due to the remarkable feature of Minkowski's inquiry, in that he grasps them in terms of lived experience in all its emotive and imaginary shapes, that he opens the door not only to diagnosis but also to therapy.

3. Experiential structures of time

In general, time for Minkowski is neither the time of ordinary life, which can be measured in years or seconds, nor the time of clinicians who ask their patients how long they have spent in the hospital, or ask them to assess the duration of a certain signal. Such a definition of time covers only a small part of the time phenomenon, that of *living reality,* which he calls "lived duration" (*durée vécue*). In line with Heidegger, Minkowski expresses this not only in universal but also in concretely psychological terms. Following Bergson, he defines time as "that fluid mass, that moving, mysterious, grand and powerful ocean," [170] which he sees around himself and in himself when meditating on time. It is the universal and impersonal becoming which cannot be defined better, for it is the synonym of life in the wider meaning of the word. Becoming can best be perceived when there is no precise feeling or thought in consciousness; it is essentially an irrational phenomenon. Even the most elementary processes of discursive thought are opposed to its nature, and we can never consider it from a sufficient distance to make it an "object."

Physicists, on the other hand, are able to express time in terms of space as a succession of points, each point expressing the position of an object at a certain time. For Minkowski, such an easy representation of time would not be possible without the existence of intimate, intermediary links between the notion of time assimilated to space and the notion of duration as experienced. Assuming the two extreme aspects of time, first an irrational phenomenon, then a physical phenomenon which can be represented by a straight line, Minkowski concludes that "consequently there must be phenomena which come and intercalate themselves between these two extreme aspects of time . . ." making possible the passage from one to the other. Minkowski introduces these phenomena as irreducible psychological elements. They resist any attempt to bring them entirely to the level of rational factors; however, it should be possible to relate them to the notion of space. The novelty of these *spatio-temporal phenomena* is that we *can analyze the lived experience in terms of "time-quality" and "space-quality."* At this point we can see the significance of Minkowski's basic conception of time in experiential terms involving all psychological factors, which by its rich concreteness completes Heidegger's more universal scheme in the direction of individual differentiation, and thereby breaks through into psychological practice.

Minkowski distinguishes between time and space, "lived succession" and "lived continuity," as two dimensions of experience linked by a "principle of unfolding" (*principe de déploiement*).[171] Then he establishes the temporal norms in terms of three stages of temporality as experienced.

a. *The present and the now*

Using "now" as the attribute of being "one elementary part of a whole," Minkowski defines his notion of "present" as including and surpassing the notion of "now." In fact, the "now" is contradictory in itself for, though it is part of a whole, it does not admit of the existence of anything besides itself; thus it substitutes itself for the whole. The "present," on the contrary, is in some way impregnated with what was before, and what will come after.

b. *The future*

The notion of the future is for Minkowski much more important than the notion of the past, for the latter is nearer to being knowledge than is life because of the role played by memory. We experience the future in terms of six vital phenomena:

Activity and expectation. Activity is a temporal factor, it is "active duration" or, better, duration oriented toward the future. Its opposite is expectation, and not passivity. In a state of activity we *go toward* the future; in a state of expectation we *wait for* the future to come to us. On the other hand, the passage from expectation to activity contributes toward awakening in us "an active-sensitive surface" as a center of interaction between the I and my immediate milieu.

Desire and hope allow us to go further than activity and to widen our perspective. They are precisely the emotive factors that create for us the future, bringing us intentionally into contact with the mediate, the *not yet here*.

Prayer and ethical impulse are two higher components of

the future. Prayer, which plays the same role as hope when hope becomes impossible, is also a process of total, lived interiorization. It is what binds the present and the expected future. The ethical impulse is something most fundamental in human beings. On the one hand, the universal capacity for producing ethical actions is a basic condition for humanity. On the other hand, the future itself is nothing other than an "ideal," a pursuit of ethical action. We experience the future as an exceptional realization of what is most elevated and sublime in us. As such it is self-sufficient; and if we do not feel "up to it" at one moment, we expect to be up to it sometime, which hope belongs also to the ideal. Therefore the ethical impulse allows us to reach the sublime, and so achieve the freedom of greater self-consciousness.

These three stages of the future can also be expressed by the feelings: "I exist," taken as the coordinated structure "I-here-now," shows an intimate union of time and space; "I have" is a phenomenon of a greater amplitude than the "I exist," for it tends to increase the sphere of our being by surrounding it with the larger sphere of our "having." The third feeling corresponding to the future, "I belong to," is brought about by the ethical impulse and enables us to situate ourselves before mankind. It extends my horizon beyond myself, my social group, etc., toward all humanity. It is only by orienting our *élan vital* toward this vast perspective that we grow and experience universal unfolding of our potentialities (*épanouissement*).

That is how orientation toward the future gives meaning to life. Where it is missing everything seems senseless, indifferent, stupid. The vital impulse is either exhausted of its force or entirely suppressed.

c. *The past*

For Minkowski, "memory" cannot account completely for the phenomenon of the past since it does not enable us to choose with certainty between the two propositions: "we remember what has been" and "what has been has been only because we remember it." And yet we choose the first without any hesitation. We must then admit a primitive intuition of the past, independent of concrete memory. This notion, in opposition to a rational conception of memory, opens the way to a phenomenology of the past. The past is a projection into what has once been but now lies behind, inert, deprived of its own dynamics of the *élan vital*. The past is therefore essentially static. As in the experience of the future, we find three steps in the experience of the past: "remorse-regret-ordinary memory." Yet the analogy is not complete, for, while in the future the farthest step or ethical search was the richest, in the past the farthest step is, on the contrary, the poorest phenomenon and ends in the night of oblivion.

The normal phenomenon of spatio-temporal structure gives predominance to the future towards which the vector of the structures of the *élan vital* with all its emotive, imaginative and rational forms is oriented. The various ways in which the natural *equilibrium* among the three stages of time is distorted corresponds, as we will attempt to show, to various kinds of mental diseases.

4. *Spatio-temporal norms in psycho-therapy*

(*The methodological shift from one outstanding symptom | in classic psychology | to the fundamental basis of all symptoms.*)

After this brief account of the general conception of time as experienced, let us now see some examples of its application to the treatment of mental diseases. Its fundamental methodological devices are derived from the conception of "mental automatism," introduced by de Clérambault and referred to by Minkowski. In opposition to classical psychiatry, de Clérambault considers that two levels of phenomena of disease should be distinguished: the initial manifestation or mental automatism as the fundamental syndrome and a secondary intellectual construction which alone should take the name of true mania. In opposition to classical psychology (Bleuler), de Clérambault understands as the fundamental syndrome not a mere association of symptoms "but the expression of a deep characteristic modification of the whole human personality." Consequently, the psychiatrist must reach, through the ideational and emotional elements of a syndrome, the ultimate structure of the morbid personality, which as a "generator of disorder" (*troubles générateurs*) is its basis. Mignard distinguishes two fundamental distorted structures as generators of disorder: "spatial mental subduction" and "temporal mental subduction" as motivating respectively the degradation of the personality in space (*e.g.,* syndrome of de Clérambault), and the degradation of the personality in time (e.g., melancholic delirium).

a. *Loss of contact with reality*

Introducing the concept of the syndrome as referring, not to any particular symptom (as Bleuler, faithful to classic psychology, does), but to the generating disorder as a basic distortion of the spatio-temporal structure, Minkowski has offered essential clues for diagnosis and treatment of schizophrenia. The feeling "I-here-now" is an elementary and irreducible affirmation of the dynamism of life independent of all rational knowledge. Schizophrenia is precisely an expression of its deformation, which Minkowski—grasping the entire syndrome—defines as "loss of contact with reality" in terms of space and time.

For instance, a general paralytic will answer to the question, "Where are you?" by saying "Here," without being able to remember any fact about the place. A schizophrenic, on the contrary, will answer that he knows where he is but cannot relate himself to it, or that the expressions "to be," "to exist," do not mean anything to him. To the question, "Where do you come from?" the general paralytic would answer, "From where I was before," showing that he still has the power of perceiving changes of place; while to the question, "Where are you?" the senile insane would answer, "I have been here since this morning," using a purely imaginary temporal factor to reinforce his affirmation. The schizophrenic, on the contrary, seems more and more a prisoner of purely spatial relations. He often replaces the adverbs such as "when" with spatial adverbs such as "where." Fisher expresses this phenomenon by saying that the temporal elements of the schizophrenic are more and more imbued with internal spatiality; essentially rational and static spatial elements suppress his vital dynamism, weaken his "lived duration," and provoke "morbid rationalism." A schizophrenic loses all vital contact with reality while becoming prisoner of a perfectly static, rational universe.

b. *Disintegration of the notion of time; predominance of the "now."*

Diseases characterized by the "temporal subduction" as a generator of disorder are more difficult to analyze than the preceding ones. In general they are defined by a degradation of the power of affective union with the surroundings (*syntonia*). Bleuler seeks the roots of the weakened syntonia in an intense interior activity. This explanation, however, is unsatisfactory since interior activity lacks the necessary bearing upon individual feelings to cause one's detachment from the surroundings. Minkowski analyzes this phenomenon in terms of the vital impulse, of the lived duration; for sufferings have to be spread over a certain time and syntonia is, at the limit, the power of sharing the sufferings of others. While sympathy with others is taking place, syntonia establishes a harmony between our own duration and that of others; as an element of lived synchronism, syntonia would be a positive quality. Therefore, in case of disturbance, it seems that it is rather a modification within syntonia itself that takes place than a modification of degree, as classic psychology would suggest. The nature of this modification appears clearly in a case of maniac excitement. Unlike a schizophrenic, the patient remains in contact with reality, but the contact is instantaneous; he lacks orientation in time; he has no present—he lies in the "now." To the question, "Are you happy?" the patient answers, "Where? Now? I do not know." The notion of present has been completely replaced by that of "now," which does not relate the patient either to past experiences or to hopes, desires, and aspirations pointing toward the future. Such a patient could be treated by fixing his attention on the past, thus liberating him from a deviation of his psychological life which is entirely dominated by the disconnected "now." This disconnectedness motivates the instantaneous character of his experiences and is a foundation for his excited state.

c. *An example of complete disintegration of the notion of time.*

Minkowski gives us the example of a young man of twenty-six presenting a complete case of disintegration of the notion of time. The patient had received a college education and could analyze himself very well. The symptoms of his mental disorder can be grouped in several categories, each representing a special aspect of the disease.[172]

The patient tells us first of a feeling of displacement towards the rhythm of general becoming. "I feel time flying away, but I don't have the sensation of following it; I feel as if I were revolving contrariwise to the earth. I feel that time goes away very quickly, more quickly than for others, and that is an atrocious feeling. . . ." For Minkowski this last sentence is a confirmation of his theory that the "experienced synchronism" between our activity and general becoming constitutes an indivisible whole so that, when it is lacking, not only have we a feeling of staying behind, but becoming loses its normal rhythm and returns to its primitive and chaotic form, creating in us the feeling of "an animal fear" referred to by the patient.

If we neglect some complaints of a spatial order, such as an incapacity to assimilate the movement of things, we come then to a group of sentences showing a loss of the sensation of continuity. "At each moment I live I have the sensation of having just fallen from heaven. . . . When I do something, I have the impression of doing it for the last time." We have here a good example of a patient who has lost perception of the notion of the present, and is living entirely in the "now," as we have already defined it.

"I feel time flowing away, but I have no notion at all of the value of the time which has gone. The whole year that I've been sick means nothing precise to me." Our patient has lost the feeling of participating as a contemporary in surrounding events. This notion of participation has nothing to do with the notion of presence; it is directly linked to the notions of "lived duration" and of experienced synchronism. It would be the same thing to say, in Bergson's words, that the patient can no longer live "what is new at each moment of history." Though we wake up every morning, each morning we have the impression of starting a new day. If these days are too similar, we are bored, which is still a living phenomenon since it shows a desire for something else. Our patient is not even bored; he has a feeling of "eternity"; he feels in a state of lethargy.

Stopped in his own dynamism, our patient seems also to have lost the faculty of perceiving the movement of things around him. "I can see a tree, but I cannot see a car in motion." Our eyes are not enough to assure the perception of motion. We must also be able to relate the visual images of motion to a feeling of "experienced duration," a feeling which our patient no longer possesses. As a consequence he has the impression that he is living in the "now." The "past" and the "future" are no longer linked together. "I am in the present only by thought, but neither by feeling nor by emotivity. I am obsessed with the past . . . I have a tendency to link everything to the past." The future has disappeared too. "When I speak about the future, it is without being conscious of it; the future means nothing to me." The function of dynamic integration, which normally makes us feel that our present is a consequence of our past and that our projects will spring out of our present, has disappeared. Our consciousness of time is made up of two distinct elements, one dynamic and the other of a more static nature, which are intimately linked together in informal life. The generative disorder of our patient seems to be that he cannot unite what can exist only as united.

The feeling of fatality, of being ineluctably "too late," seems to be linked to this conception of the future, which becomes a mere reacting of the past.

M. M. Straus and Gebsattel have particularly studied the modifications of time phenomenon in states of melancholy depression. Straus starts from Honigswald's opposition between immanent and transitive time, the latter being the time we live in common with other people, and differing from physical time in that it admits of elective points such as "now," "today," "yesterday."

These two modes can be in a state of harmony, but more often they disagree. Sometimes our immanent time seems to progress faster than transitive time, and we feel happy and cheerful; sometimes it seems to lag behind, and we are bored and sad. In pathological states, and particularly in cases of endogenous depression, the opposition between the two modes becomes striking. The progressing of immanent time seems to stop altogether—as a direct consequence, according to Straus, of a biological disorder. So the biological cause and the consequent inhibition can be put together in a single conceptual unit. What is the consequence of this lack of concordance between our two modes of time? Our life is essentially oriented toward the future; when a psychological slowdown takes place either the present or the past will take on an undue importance in our psychological life.

d. *A case observed by Gebsattel is given by Minkowski as corroborating Straus's theory.*

The patient is a girl of twenty, afflicted with endogenous melancholy. Here are some significant sentences: "All day long I feel anxious about time. I cannot help thinking incessantly that time passes. Now, while speaking to you, I think, when pronouncing each word: past, past, past. I cannot understand how other people have projects and link them with precise moments of time and remain perfectly calm while so doing. For that reason I feel like a stranger toward others, as if I were no longer a member of the community. . . ."

To analyze this case, Gebsattel contrasts his "constructive

genetic method" with the "historico-genetic method" which would simply try to explain, by studying the past of the patient, why her attention is so focused on time. The life of the patient, normally oriented toward the future in relation to the constant progression of the vital impulse, has been deeply modified by an inhibition: time now seems to be only passing, ineluctably flying away. Dominated by that aspect of time, the patient perceives all outside facts in this light. Her immanent time having stopped in some way, the outside facts perceived in this light seem to her to be in perfect logical concordance with her own mood. She has a strong feeling of logic, truth, increase of knowledge, and superiority to others.

Our life has meaning only on account of its orientation towards the future; when that orientation disappears the question "Why all that?" comes to the mind, creating a state of anxiety. The fear of death is another aspect of the same phenomenon, with its paradoxical consequence, the tendency to suicide in order to escape from the fear of death.

e. A case of schizophrenic melancholy. Disintegration of the vital impulse and of the notion of the future[173]

Minkowski now gives us the example of a patient of sixty-six, in a state of melancholy delirium with extensive ideas of persecution and an elaborate interpretation of them by the patient. The patient, being of foreign origin, sees a crime without equal in the fact that he has not chosen French nationality, a crime for which he is going to receive an atrocious punishment. His arms and legs will be cut off, a nail will be driven through his head and his body will be filled with rubbish. With the exception of his family, who will share his fate, the whole country is conspiring against him, saving all the trash they can for the day of his execution: hair, nails, empty bottles, old papers, water, rotten fruit, everything. . . .

There is nothing very special in this clinical description except the extent, almost the universality, of the patient's interpretation. With a more limited symptom, we would be more interested in the reasons for its limitation, that is to say in its content, which modern psychiatry would explain by such notions as complexes, affective factors, or symbolism. In the case of our patient, on the contrary, when the morbid phenomenon has a character of universality, we are led to study it in itself, as a specific and unique phenomenon. For Minkowski the most significant points of the diagnosis were the following phenomenological factors: the mental disorder of the patient seems to be conditioned by a difference in rhythms between his psychological life and ours. But what is the origin of this difference? The psychological structures of each seem so different that it is difficult at first to find any points of contact between them. Yet modern psychiatry helps us to trace many morbid manifestations back to normal factors.

On the first evening, the patient declares that his execution will take place that night. Minkowski then thinks it will be easy to show him the next day that, since nothing has happened, he can now sleep quietly every night. But our patient is incapable of that empirical deduction typical of a normal mind. He has lost the feeling of "experienced duration," and for him there is only a juxtaposition of unrelated elements. All days are gray and similar. No desire can have its origin in the present and reach toward the future. The past cannot be used, for the notion of necessary progression has been lost. The future is barred by the certitude of a dreadful event, and all the patient's energy is fixed on that point in the future, thus destroying his whole temporal structure, that is to say, the most important aspect of his vital impulse.

Only two factors remain, the self and a hostile universe. In that perspective delirious ideas are no longer products of a morbid imagination but an effort to translate the new situation with which the disintegrating personality is confronted into the language used before the disease.

f. *Compensation and imagination*

Élan vital in its evolutive emerging is, according to Minkowski, subjected to two essential deformations: loss of dynamism and limitation. Both of them refer to some deformations of spatio-temporal forms, for example, senile fabulation is attributed to the loss of relationship with the past: lack of memory. Psychological insanity will consist of some form of compensation which substitutes for the deformed elements of the spatio-temporal structure.

Minkowski distinguishes three different forms of compensation: *affective* compensation, *mechanical* compensation and *phenomenological* compensation. Minkowski rejects the particular insistence on affective compensation, whose protagonists, fascinated by the causal genesis, attempt to explain disease in terms of the purely affective content and thereby arbitrarily subordinate the entire human being to one of his aspects, making of him *homo libidinosus,* like *homo sapiens* or *homo economicus* alone. This oversimplified approach to man at a certain moment bars the way leading toward understanding man in his entirety. On the contrary, if we consider the relations between the emotive factors and the spatio-temporal data furnished by the psychological syndrome, we arrive at a more complete conception of compensation—*phenomenological* compensation.

Phenomenological compensation is best studied by Minkowski in schizophrenics. This affliction is characterized mainly by a loss of vital contact with reality. The schizophrenic will then have a tendency to seek refuge in moods which in normal life are reactions of retreat, such as dreams, regrets, and interrogations. He will tend to organize them in an ideo-emotive or ideo-affective expression. Here, however, while Bleuler along with classical psychology will look for one outstanding, meaningful expression, Minkowski is looking for the unifying foundation of all of them. It is not in the interpretative ideational meaning that he will search for the generating trouble but, leaving aside the former completely, he finds it in the way in which the living individual situates himself with respect to time and space.

As we have already mentioned, the different types of compensation are achieved through the exercise of imagination by the patient. Since, on the other hand, most of the mental diseases are characterized by the impoverishment or the deformation of one of the three constituents—past-present-future—of lived duration, it seems that the pathologist will have to direct his efforts toward helping the patient to rebuild his spatio-temporal perspective by an adequate stimulation of his imaginative activity.

5. *Spatio-temporality of emotive functions; verticality of psychic life*

The new perspective of psychology and psychotherapy, as established by Minkowski and the previously mentioned group of researchers and practitioners, demands as its necesssary counterpart the corresponding exploration of the imaginative, emotive and rational sources of man's vital commitment, as materials out of which his self-including world is constructed.

Among various studies in this field, the most outstanding

example of the existential-anthropological approach along the lines previously mentioned is offered by R. Desoille and Gaston Bachelard. Bachelard's inquiry into the field of creative imagination, its sources, emotive value and schemes of translation into rational interpretation through symbols, and the therapeutic method of Desoille, based upon the recognition of imagination as a ground of emotivity, offer jointly a complete insight into psychological motivation; they mark a turning point in psychology. Initially inspired by Desoille's therapeutic method, which has been widely used in Switzerland, both of these enterprises take their starting point from three insights. First of all, a distinction is made between *representational* and *creative* imagination. While the first consists merely in the reproduction of perception, the second "constitutes an autochthonous kingdom." Reference is made to the view of Max Scheler, who, opposing the Freudian conception of sublimation, affirms that the entire emotive universe cannot be reduced to natural drives, that the metaphors of the creative imagination are irreducible to concupiscence, etc. On the contrary, the creative imagination escapes all psychological determination; it has a source of its own. As such, it is itself the most basic factor of all psychological creativity (activity). Translating Heidegger's basic conception of being-in-the-world into specific psychological terms, it can be said that "psychologically we are created by our imagination (*rêverie*); created and limited, because it is creative imagination (*rêverie*) that determines the farthest borderlines of our spirit." [174] Experience of philosophy, science and poetry is reconciled in this most significant recognition, which Bachelard expresses by quoting Novalis: "From creative imagination should be derived all the faculties, all the activities of (man's) *exterior and interior world*." Imagination is the force of psychological creativity more than will and more than *élan vital;* inversely, these two latter appear in the inquiries of Bachelard and Desoille as having their dynamic source precisely in imagination.

Furthermore, in this perspective, imagination appears as the center not only of our energies but also of the equilibrium between the self and the world; it is from this center that emerge the two directions of all psychological ambivalence, extroversion and introversion.

Imagination works in terms of metaphors. Therefore, the secret of mutating human energies is to be found in *image dreaming* (*rêverie*), transforming forms previously transformed and so on *ad infinitum*. It is precisely through the decomposing of metaphors that an image becomes psychologically active.

What is the origin of creative imagination? Referring to C. G. Jung's theory of *archetypes* of imagination as the ultimate anthropological condition of humanity, Bachelard and Desoille search for it in the primitive intellectual evidences which naturally arise from primitive images we form, and the impressions that suddenly give interest to something that did not have it before—the object—making it "valuable." In this sense the image precedes the object—imagination precedes perception. Although, parallel with Jung, the primitive ground of the first images is conceived in terms of four fundamental material substances, dividing types of images with respect to specific potentialities which they possess to inspire specific types of images, Bachelard completely reorients the direction attributed to imagination and even culture as such. This general insight challenges the assumptions of realistic philosophy and common psychology that it is the perception of images that determines the processes of imagination: "first to see things, then to imagine them." In this conception, says Bachelard, imagination is reduced to a faculty of combining fragments of previously perceived reality, the remembrances of experienced reality. This assumption alone precludes the possibility of attaining the realm of the essentially creative imagination.[175] While the key to a realistically understood culture is to *have seen much* and seen well, following C. G. Jung, Bachelard says the key is "to dream well and faithfully to the oneirism of the archetypes, which are rooted in the deepest realm of man's unconsciousness."

The imagined images are sublimations of the archetypes rather than reproductions of reality; there are root-metaphors first; from them follow series of metaphors in a progressive transformation. It is through this dialectical process of sublimation—the most fundamental psychological process—that esthetic values are developed. In a way, as can be seen from the fact that it is in the realm of art that the images are most clearly exhibited, this entire process of metaphoric transformation is an esthetic process. Thus evidence is revealed for the interesting statement that esthetic values are indispensable to normal psychical activity. It is expected that their reference to the four material substances with the ultimate intellectual evidences which they inspire—corresponding to what C. G. Jung calls "collective unconscious" as the manifestation of the "deeper strata of unconscious where remain sleeping the ancestral images belonging to the whole of humanity" [176]—will confer universal validity on the patterns of images established in this inquiry.

But, corresponding to Bergson's insight[177] that there is a previous selection which establishes itself among all possible components of the image dream in the function of one of them that plays the role of a principal conductor of the image dream, the main objective of this research and also the key to its application consists in establishing the patterns of their succession.

Desoille has laid foundations for the orientation of the inquiry and has developed the therapeutics of image dreaming; Bachelard completes it, first by furnishing ample material and then by establishing (in terms of images and their relation) the fundamental union among all psychological faculties. The rotating axis, however, of this original approach consists in the revolutionary insight of Desoille that the entire universe of emotions, moods, imagination, will, courage, etc., is of a spatio-temporal, *vertical character*. As the following chapters will attempt to illustrate by examples taken from Bachelard's analysis, imagination, the motor of all psychical forces, follows a *vertical* line in correspondence to them.

Examples of imagination as a fundamental creative force; as a source unifying all psychological faculties.

The four fundamental material elements which Bachelard considers to be the ultimate points of reference for creative imagination are: fire, air, water and earth. Through the types of images they inspire, they become junctions between imagination and other psychological faculties; and since the created images are respectively situated along the vertical, they can be translated in terms or factors of "rise" or "fall." In general, the images of air have an essentially uplifting tendency; the images of fire a dynamic and vitalizing tendency, etc.; the images of solid substances of the earth, whether hard like metal, stone, rubber, wood, etc., or soft like dough or mud, have especially rich psychological ramifications in terms of energy and activity.

In particular the solid, hard substances establish, according to Bachelard, a junction between imagination and will in terms of courage, perseverance, force, etc. Bachelard says, "We do not want anything but what we richly (abundantly) imagine." [178] As a matter of fact, when we see and touch solid materials, they awake in us the feeling of resistance, which gives rise to a dynamic reaction, a drive toward action. It is by feeling the resistance of hard matter that a child first becomes aware of his dynamic powers. The classical psychologist, says Bachelard, will object that the first resistance a child experiences comes from his parents, that the resistances which bind our psyche are in general social. Against the "ephemeral" social bias of psychoanalysis, Bachelard presents experiential evidence that it is the feeling of resistance, which is at the basis of the virile satisfaction of carving hard materials, which is to be considered in relation to sadistic instincts. For example, there is a special image-dreaming enjoyment in exercising our force with a sharp surgical blade over the skin, carving with a certain skill a scientific furrow in the flesh—"the spirit rejoices, while the flesh suffers." There is also an imaginative coordination between the form of carved furrows and the form of lines. A child carving a reed pipe obliquely is already realizing human disloyalty. These evidences of conditioning our unconscious tendencies directly by images, awakened in contact with matter, displaces the main source of inhibitions from the social realm to that of the imagination of material substances.

There is a well known symbolic expression of the feeling of power and dynamic strength, awakened by the imagination of massive, heavy loads, in terms of the will meeting their resistance experienced as a provocation. A mountain, for example, possesses the character of crushing majesty by its imposing weight, to which corresponds a psychological "heaviness." To understand well the massiveness of a mountain one has to imagine lifting it. Imaginatively it represents a crushing cosmos. At the psychological level it can be represented by an "absolute irremediable," as for example in Flaubert's *Salammbô,* when the expression is used, "It was as if mountains weighed over my days." This psychological heaviness of the imagination of crushing can awaken either submission or resistance. The challenge of weight awakens force and the will to measure up to it. This phenomenon is at the basis of the myth of Atlas lifting the earth. It focuses the will to resist the crushing of destiny. If we come to realize images of weight, we will love to carry loads. In the literal sense a child likes to carry a bag; figuratively, we are willing to carry the heavy burdens of everyday life. The myth of Sisyphus is equally the myth of the mountain. Realizing in rich images the resistance of an uplifted mountain will provoke an energy and a persevering will to lift it. It does not matter that there will be no decisive victory over the load, that we will fall under it each evening. We will start next morning all over again with fresh strength as we do with the burdens of life.

As a sort of cosmic moral, the great spectacles of nature teach man how not to succumb to the heavy loads, the strenuous fights, how to keep his head high and to continue courageously his everyday work. Bachelard attributes the cosmic dynamism of Victor Hugo to the impulses given in his work by a frequent image of the fight between massive rocks and the ocean. The recurrent image of the rock resisting ever renewed assaults awakens a dynamic force and the will to persevere in the hardship of life, the courage to continue the fight, the will to endure. In his "Essay on Nature" Emerson says: "Who knows how much of fortitude has the rock beaten by the sea taught the fisherman?"

To contemplate the union of the imagination with material forces means to fight with all human efforts against all oppressing natural forces. This is also the meaning of the myth of Hercules' labors.

Myths and mythology appear as groups of rich images. Herein lies their twofold meaning. First, myths or their fragments express the rationalized meaning of the imaginative fixation of the unconscious. Second, it would constitute a practice of hygiene for the mind to study the rich, splendid, legendary images, for example, of Hercules' efforts, in their imaginative dynamism. These splendid lyrical images would raise the tone of the whole human being.

To summarize, images of massive, heavy matter have an uplifting character. The forces they awake tend "upward," they lift us and encourage us to walk with head high.

On the opposite side, Bachelard places the images of falling. He tells us of an accident in his unconscious life that occurred when he visited the tower of the Strasbourg cathedral. At a certain point the ascent was so abrupt that he experienced complete vertigo. From that moment in his unconscious life there remained engraved a presentiment of a fall, an immense fall which, at the slightest suggestion, in dream as well as in reality, caused an infinite malaise to seize him. H. Steffers defines vertigo as a sudden and irremediable solitude.[179] Once it takes possession of a person, he will fall; nothing he may lean upon, no hand he may grasp, can prevent him from falling. He is seized in the innermost center of his being, and nothing can save him; he feels himself a living fall. This fall opens abysses in his being. It is a destruction of his being. It suffices to feel the presentiment of a fall to awake trembling from a dream.

This imaginary experience of falling shows with particular clarity the independence of imagination from reality, its autonomous origin. The images of falling, in fact, surpass actual experience and give a permanent reality to ephemeral dangers, even if we never actually experience a fall. They tend to dramatize the fall, to make of it a destiny, a type of death. Bachelard refers to Maria Montessori, who emphasized that a newborn infant, when there is any instability of our hold upon him, may already fear a fall. This clearly illustrates the general conception that the creative imagination is the most fundamental source of psychological activity.

In general, abysmal, infernal images have, in the light of the previous analysis, a paralyzing and destructive character.

There is, however, a dialectic between the images of falling and of rising or lifting. Loads fall, we fall, and we want to lift them and ourselves. Bachelard sees this will to redress the fall as a special anthropological dialectic and a sublimating function of the human psyche: to keep the head high.

In general, as we have seen, matter reveals our forces to us. It also suggests an organization of our forces in dynamic categories. This leads further to a most revelatory insight into our work on solid matter. From the contact with matter emerges, first of all, the will to work on it. An actual work on matter means, however, an opening into a twofold perspective: *toward the inner life of the working subject and toward the interior of the object.* The inquiring contact with the substance gives an imaginative illusion of attaining its ground—a horizon of unknown riches opens. It is toward this unlimited and rich domain that the acting subject extends and projects, his hitherto encapsulated, limited inner life. While working, these two poles—the subject's interior and the substance—change places, and in the being of the workman there develops a salutary rhythm of introversion and extroversion. Imagination thus appears as the center from which arise these two directions of the entire psychical life, introversion and extroversion.

In short, the direction "downward," through images of morbid heaviness, solitude, infernal myths, suppressed efforts, etc., leads toward a fall; the direction "upward," proceeding by images of flight, energy, will, courage, perseverance, etc., leads to a lifting up. Thus, an agreement with the most intimate intuition of Minkowski, the dynamic images of energy, will and force—symbols of *élan vital* and rising up—are oriented toward the future, as an open, unlimited field of action, while the direction downward through the gradual images of suppression, limitation and inertia constitutes an orientation toward the static past.

6. *The therapeutic method of image-dreaming*[180]

Here lies the crucial point of Desoille's therapeutic of image-dreaming. Both classic psychoanalysis and Desoille's method of image-dreaming work in terms of symbols. However, the most remarkable feature of symbolism as interpreted by Desoille is the association of visual and affective images with the moving images of ascent and descent. All types of symbolism are concentrated around this axis.

It is precisely the ascending direction taken by the method of image-dreaming that constitutes its main novelty. In a way Freudian psychoanalysis also relies upon the verticality of our emotive subconscious; however, the different direction of its procedure defines the fundamental difference in the objectives of classic psychoanalysis and the methods of Bachelard and Desoille. As a matter of fact, psychoanalysis, in order to unknot the complexes, is oriented "downward"; while making the patient progressively reactualize his past, it leads him to the hidden "abysmal" springs of his unconscious life. This descent, as Bachelard remarks, is difficult. Patients with disturbing phenomena in the inferior strata of their psyches show a strong resistance against descending toward them, which constitutes one of the main difficulties of the treatment and often prolongs it. By unknotting the complexes in the revival of past experience, the patient is supposed to be freed from the morbid symptoms by a voluntary abandoning of the morbid tendencies motivated by the complex. No new salutary tendencies are, however, substituted by this therapy. Desoille's procedure of image-dreaming activated in an ascending direction is first of all directly oriented to combating the resistances provoked by inhibitions and to finding the hidden tendency, not by searching in the past for the initiating complex, but by making the patient live new experiences —sentiments, emotions. Instead of making the patient sacrifice his tendencies, which until now he considers legitimate, Desoille substitutes for them the vision of satisfaction, the uncovering of the patient's most noble tendencies, implying thereby another, a new, conception of happiness. Because of this feature, Desoille calls it the "method of sublimation." Thus, while psychoanalysis is oriented towards the past, the method of image-dreaming anticipates the future, touching thereby the "abysmal psychology of the self" which Freud thought of as inaccessible to direct study by analysis.

The technique of image-dreaming proceeds at five levels, established according to the natural place that images occupy on the vertical. They should be read from the last number downward:

5. The fifth level consists of mystico-celestial images corresponding to purely euphoric emotions of universal harmony, beatitude, peace, optimism, etc.;

4. Images of universal mythology corresponding to universal and highly elevated tendencies and emotions;

3. Images of the personal unconscious revealing the patient's hidden tendencies;

2. Images of inferior mythology, in which the patient's actual state is either directly expressed, or his potentialities are directly stimulated;

1. Images of infernal mysticism expressing the "abysmal" springs of his morbid tendencies.

The technique—which Desoille calls an "art," since it demands a great amount of invention and personal experience by the analyst—starts, after a general relaxation is induced by muscular exercises, with the suggestion of the first image.

Through the modification, spontaneous or suggested, of the first image, an ascension is obtained. For example, Desoille suggested the image of flowers to a patient. The patient immediately imagined a field of rippling grain mixed with daisies. The field lay on the side of a hill bathed in sunshine. The analyst asked whether it was a simple reminiscence of nature or whether the image contained a symbol. The patient answered that he interpreted it as a "promise of days when serenity will be combined and blended with a rich spiritual harvest." Instead of giving the patient—as psychoanalysts do—a detailed analysis of these symbols, since his aim is not to revive the past but to anticipate the future, Desoille suggested that the patient transpose this image to several gradually more elevated levels until the flowers become only shining colorful phantoms. At this level the patient experienced a feeling of intense freshness and purity; he could not, however, ascend any farther, fearing that in the next region there would be no more forms. Desoille then suggested that he imagine some "useful diversion" in order to provoke auto-criticism leading to a revelation of his main trouble. Expounding the trouble, his intense emotive dynamism was liberated. Then Desoille suggested that he summon up in one image all the persons who, as it had been revealed, oppressed the patient. "I evoke them, and all evil vanishes. There are no longer the offender and the offended. There are only creatures harmonized to the divine rhythm. Each being takes on a precious value."

Before the dynamism of this image is exhausted, the patient is supposed to find a new symbol. This time, it is a sword hanging in the sky—"the sword of justice," which gives the patient an experience of ultimate peace, beauty and harmony. Whatever other meanings this symbol may have (it has an erotic value in psychoanalysis), here it has taken the value of universal harmony. The aim is achieved: the patient has substituted for the images of events formed by instincts, the image of wisdom, which, reproduced in every appropriate circumstance, becomes a directive in his life.

Of course in actual analysis, after this symbol is fixed, Desoille suggests to the patient images of descent until he reaches his normal state, feeling, however, refreshed, optimistic and peaceful. By transposing the image of flowers to various higher levels the work of sublimation is begun, by which is meant a reorientation of attention towards images inspiring optimism, activity, etc. With the suggestion of ascension is connected the representation of the most generous and constructive possibilities of the patient. The return by a descending succession of images, recalling the principal images from the start in inverse order, followed by a brief recollection of the accepted suggestions, ends with images of good health. It is the suggested and controlled ascending direction of the procedure that constitutes the novelty of this method. As Pierre Janet formulates it, the patient has mobilized the deep energies of his superior psychism in order to maintain himself at a desired level of equilibrium. This method is considered by Desoille as a conscious sublimation. For old, instinctive inhibitions, new, conscious inhibitions are substituted. Bachelard insists that inhibited conscious activity is not only not harmful, but even a necessary condition for scholarship, concentration, and culture in general.

7. *"Existential" psychoanalysis*

In our survey of current trends in psychology and psychopathology—insofar as they result from new, original themes, together with their formulations in contemporary continental philosophy—we cannot omit Jean-Paul Sartre's conception of "existential" psychoanalysis. Sartre's conception of psychoanalysis is based on philosophical assumptions which can be considered as a synthesis of the acquisitions of contemporary philosophy. In this work the sharp distinction between the contemporary philosophical attitude and the naturalistic presuppositions of Freud's theory, typical for the end of the nineteenth century, have become apparent. In spite of the similarities between Sartrean and Freudian theories of psychoanalysis, Sartre's theory gives the most representative picture of the differences in practice resulting from the basically different philosophical presuppositions of contemporary thought and those at the end of the nineteenth century.

An outgrowth of Sartre's philosophy (phenomenological ontology), Sartre's theory of psychoanalysis is founded on the conception of man's *being-in-the-world,* a conception which Sartre shares with Heidegger.[181] However, Sartre's doctrine constitutes an original and penetrating variation on several of the themes of Heidegger's ontology of man. Although it does not seem that this view has gained acceptance in psychopathological *praxis,* the philosophical ideas which it synthesizes have pervaded general discussion, if not in clinical psychoanalysis, certainly in the currently popular "literary psychoanalysis" focused on exceptional individuals and their "destinies." It is this completeness which justifies mention of Sartre's inquiry in this survey.

It would be a misunderstanding of Sartre's credo if we were to judge the interest or validity of his method by the criterion of clinical efficiency. On the contrary, Sartre takes up Max Scheler's criticism of classical psychoanalysis as a doctrine which creates its notions exclusively on the basis of and for the sake of pathological cases. He follows Gaston Bachelard in the conception of an "objective psychoanalysis" which would be a method of helping a normal individual to clarify the origin and nature of his emotive and intellectual life. Such an "objective psychoanalysis" would thus serve as a tool for rectifying emotive and intellectual life, issuing from unclarified, instinctive sources, by the use of criteria resulting from the rational, clear recognition of facts and their significance. So far for Bachelard; Sartre himself, however, as we shall see, aims "higher."

In his major philosophical work, *Being and Nothingness*, while analyzing "bad faith" as a specific phenomenon (an insincerity of the individual's attitude toward himself) which hinders his understanding of himself (and also of the Other), Sartre attempts to establish the major point of his doctrine.[182] Following the contemporary trend of Max Scheler, Jaspers, and others, Sartre denies that man, in his entirety or in the "human reality" of his life, can be expressed by, or identified with, his conduct.[183] "I" will always tend to *refuse* to be defined and judged by a series of my acts, which, organized in a consistent pattern, will appear to make up my personality. Such a definition negates my freedom, while it attempts to construct a being for me, as if I were a thing, from the essence of which would follow all my acts. Sartre expresses this refusal in his famous formula that "existence precedes essence," which gave rise to the misinterpretations of the so-called popular "existentialism." When "existence" means undetermined freedom, it could be said, rather, that the human being does not possess any essence in the classical sense in which "essence" means determining nature. Conversely, all my acts, feelings, and so on, and also my individual reality itself, can be defined only by the ultimate aim to which they are directed. In fact, it is only in the perspective of this transcendent goal that all my acts take on a symbolic significance, from which the over-all meaningfulness of my total life in all its manifestations arises. This, then, is my *human reality*—in contradistinction to the brute physical reality of nature.

Following a similar inspiration, empirical psychology considers that the particular man can be identified with the totality of his desires, taken as a constellation of natural tendencies and organized synthetically in such a way that each of them influences all the others. However, Sartre makes a sharp distinction between the position of empirical psychology and his own. Empirical psychology first of all makes an attempt to fix the focus of its analysis at a point early in the history of the individual. Secondly, as Sartre formulates it, empirical psychology attempts to "reduce the complex personality of an adolescent to some first desires, the way a chemist reduces composites to simple bodies." [184] Sartre explains, for instance, that in the case of Flaubert empirical psychology recognizes great ambition, the need of great actions and emotions, and so on, as simple elements, which are supposed to have produced in Flaubert a "permanent state of exaltation," as shown by his correspondence.[185] Flaubert's particular personal destiny, his "literary disposition" itself, is supposed thus to be explained. It is supposed, in particular, that his destiny would follow from his literary disposition.

Sartre has two major objections to this approach, which define his own attitude. In the first place, how can the concrete fact of Flaubert's literary genius—and lack, for instance, of choreographic ability—be produced by a combination of universal, abstract laws? Why did these established desires, typical in every adolescent, produce "exaltation" in Flaubert and not, say, "impatience"? And why, asks Sartre, should a literary disposition emerge from this exaltation and not an adventurer's? Obviously inadequate for answering these questions, such universal types of desires fail to capture the concrete individual.

In the second place, the desires and tendencies in this scheme are referred to some ultimate and also unexplainable feature, such as Flaubert's ambition. According to empirical psychology, ambition, in this example, was determined: Flaubert "was like that: ambitious." We touch here upon the hub of Sartre's ideas. This ambition, according to Sartre, was not "given" to Flaubert; neither heredity nor his social condition, nor education, nor his "nervous temperament" can account for it. This ambition is "free"; it emerges from the realm of the absolute freedom of the individual. The main question would still be: what is the significance of the nature and emergence of Flaubert's ambition so that it becomes meaningful in the explanation of Flaubert's particular "destiny"? In fact, Sartre rectifies the empirical attitude: if we attempt to find out what Flaubert (the Other) is, we look for a "real irreducible." A hypothetical construction by a psychologist will not make us love or hate this man; but if we are to love or hate him, we must realize his unique, individual, concrete and immediately evident, *reality*. With reference to Heidegger's conception of man's fundamental constituent, his being-in-the-world, such an irreducible, concrete and unique factor identifying a man is seen by Sartre in man's individual uniqueness as his *original projection of his being*.

Coinciding with Heidegger's view, this original projection of man's being, on the one hand, unifies all of man's tendencies, acts, and so on, endowing them with significance without which they would remain but contingent and absurd facts. On the other hand, it unifies man, his conduct and his tendencies within the world. By an interesting contradistinction to Heidegger—which presents another step in the existential analysis of man—Sartre emphasizes the individual's uniqueness and concreteness against Heidegger's universal, fundamental human condition for *all* men. Sartre reverses the positions of the universal and concrete situations of man in Heidegger's view by laying stress upon *original choice*. Man's *original choice* consists in choosing to be incomparably unique, concrete, and irreplaceable. Man's choice of uniqueness, and so on, is connected with his most specific choices in accomplishing the task of becoming an entirely "different" being—*himself.* Thus, man's concern over his uniqueness is more basic than Heidegger's "authentic project," which relies upon the universal human condition (of being ultimately oriented toward death). Sartre's concrete projection of how a particular man can be uniquely different should not refer to anything else and ought to be grasped on the basis of its own evidence. Consequently, the projection cannot refer to death or life, nor to any particular feature of the human condition; the original projection of one's *being-for-himself* (le *pour-soi*) cannot be directed toward anything "but its own being." [186] At this point Sartre establishes an equivalence between man and being. "Man," Sartre says, "is fundamentally the desire for being." But being is not to be understood as in the classical conception, as a universal, abstract concept, but as the concrete structure of man's individual projection, symbolizing through all his empirical acts and tendencies what a man tends ultimately to become. Nevertheless, this desire for being does not exist before its expression; the desire and man's projection of it are equivalent. They are identical with man's manifold particular desires, with jealousy and avarice, the love of art and cowardice, "with the result that human reality never reveals itself to us unless manifested by *such a man,* by a particular person." [187] As a matter of fact, Sartre rejects the classical ontological distinction between the *actual* and the *possible,* where the possible precedes the actually realized (cf. Introduction to *Being and Nothingness*). There are no hidden potentialities in man preceding his actual realization, which may or may not occur. Thus, with regard to Flaubert, it may be said that his literary genius was not a latent possibility (disposition) waiting to be actualized in his literary achievements. His genius consists of those achievements, concrete elements of his concrete actual "reality" as a creative writer. Because no actual genius was ever a potential one, there are no unrealized geniuses; a genius and his destiny are his concrete reality. Since this reality is as for Heidegger, the meaningfulness of the world which defines a particular human being ultimately, it expresses itself in his original projection insofar as it expresses his free choice to be such and not another individual.

In a general exposition of Sartre's theory of psychoanalysis, Alfred Stern rightly mentions that Sartre's original projection was comparable in this respect to Alfred Adler's "life-plan." [188] Adler stresses that the "life-plan" (by which conception he attempts to express all the movements or elements constituting an individual) cannot be complete since the unifying basis is a philosophical meaningfulness. In this sense, Adler's conception is, in a way, prior to Sartre's conception of the philosophical meaningfulness of the human being and his reality. Furthermore, both of them relate this basic projection or plan to *values*, namely, to the value of the superiority of self-accomplishment. Sartre, for example, considers God as such a superior "ideal" which man strives to become.[189] Because the meaningful structure of our projection endows all our emotive, volitional and intellectual acts and tendencies with meaningfulness, it also means the "truth" of a particular human reality; moreover, it is this projection which constitutes the personality of man. One will not fail to recognize in this idea a new form of return to the classic conception of "ontological truth," as if it were building a bridge between man and being beyond cognition, yet reserving for cognition an important part in an amplified three-pole relationship.

It is by the method of existential psychoanalysis thus founded that the role of cognition in this relationship comes to light. There is a difference between merely living, or experiencing one's original projection, or truth, and having it revealed to oneself in its complete nature. The difference itself is the difference "in being." In fact, Sartre rejects the

Freudian distinction between conscious and unconscious psychological acts. Instead, as for Heidegger, all the psychological phenomena of sensibility and life mean for Sartre conscious activity. "Unconscious" is for Heidegger only the dead insensibility of inanimate nature. Furthermore, following Husserl, Sartre makes a distinction between cognitive consciousness and prereflective consciousness. In other words, although we always live our experiences with full consciousness, we do not always "know" what we experience. It is because of a special conscious activity, namely, that of *reflection,* that we come to *know* what we experience. Cognition arises only at the reflective level, while below this level we find a stream of prereflective, lived experience. Thus, we may live our original projection in full consciousness without knowing its structure, without realizing all its significance for our particular acts, and so on.

But what is the value of bringing our original projection to the level of knowledge? This value would constitute the purpose of the existential psychoanalysis. As Sartre shows, the experience of our original projection (without the conceptual knowledge of it) is not, as a Freudian would think an unsolved puzzle. On the contrary, the experience remains in "full view" and yet remains "a mystery in full view," because even the most vivid and complete experience lacks the means which permit its analysis. It grasps all at once, without putting in relief outstanding parts, without establishing proportions of greatness, value, and so on, without recognizing ramifications and ties; whereas all of this constitutes its meaningfulness. If they are not recognized, it is not because they are hidden or nonexistent, but because a more complete cognition of dimensions, proportions and connections within the original projection can be established by reflective activity which alone results in conceptual knowledge. Therefore, in the reflective reconstruction of our originally experienced projection, this projection itself is amplified, which amounts to man's explicit revelation in being. Being is, for Sartre, man's ultimate desire—its explicit revelation then constitutes man's supreme value. In a different sense, did not Socrates maintain that an unanalyzed life is not worth living?

Thus, the aim of Sartre's existential psychoanalysis is to discover and analyze man's original projection, choice or truth. As Sartre himself says in summary, the evidence and nature of this projection should be established by "phenomenological ontology," whose foundations have been outlined above. The principle of this psychoanalysis is that man is an entirety and consequently expresses himself in every act; man's innermost truth cannot help but be present in his most minute manifestation. Each of his emotive and volitive acts in all its particulars—for example, in his love for one particular woman, especially in one definite period of his life, or in a particular jealousy, and so on—is revealing of man's fundamental projection. The *aim* of this psychoanalysis is to analyze and interpret conceptually man's behavior in the largest sense of the word, in order to grasp his original projection or personality. The *starting point* of this psychoanalysis is therefore experience, and its *method* a comparison of man's various acts which should result in man's unique revelation.

Sartre makes a detailed comparison of the Freudian and his own conception of psychoanalysis with respect to the points which our study has already implicitly or explicitly covered. Perhaps it should also be mentioned that one of the main divergences in their respective presuppositions is Sartre's elimination of the libido as a factor responsible for the hidden complexities of our "unconscious" life. Sartre assumes that "bad faith" is such an instrumental factor. However, in his distinction between prereflective and conceptual knowledge (replacing Freud's distinction between conscious and unconscious life), "bad faith" hinders our self-knowledge and understanding of the reasons and meaning of our actions, but in the full light of consciousness and not in obscurity.

We cannot fail to observe in Sartre's conception of existential psychoanalysis traces of most of the insights and tendencies which have been the subject of our inquiry. As such, it offers a significant synthetic expression of the philosophical foundations of the science of man and the universe in contemporary Continental thought.

3. Concluding interpretation of results: Human reality emergent from new sources of experience.

With the anthropological conception of man's *being-in-the-world,* we have reached the apex of our inquiry. If we now return to our initial question, "What role has phenomenology played with respect to scientific investigation?", we may answer in terms of the novel responsibility phenomenologically oriented research has assumed toward man: science has again become meaningful for man's personal and human pursuits, promising him understanding on the human level instead of being concerned merely with his material comfort and physical survival. If phenomenology has fulfilled its promise of reorienting scientific research along humanly significant lines, it has done so by influencing research to turn in directions which have opened new perspectives into the nature of the universe and revealed new dimensions of human experience. These new realms of experience converge to form a philosophical world view incorporating all human pursuits into a single, essentially Human Reality.

From the beginning of Western philosophy experience has often been emphasized as the only legitimate source of testimony concerning man, the world, and man's place in the world. When Spengler's *Decline of the West*[190] appeared in the twenties it became fashionable to deplore the decline of Western culture and to accuse scientific technological industrialism of spawning a technocratic breed of man. Modern science and technology are held responsible for diverting man from the ideals of Greek, Roman, and Renaissance man, ultimately by having changed the forms of experience.

Many philosophers, among them Husserl, Jaspers and Heidegger, Merleau-Ponty and Romano Guardini, as well as sociologists like Alfred Weber and Lewis Mumford, are unanimously agreed on the chief factors which are disintegrating the Western ideal of man the "homo interior." Modern man, they agree, has lost his innermost roots in his experience of nature, his relations with others, and his awareness of his metaphysical dimension. Technocratic man, limited to conventionalized social responses and utilitarian functions designed for mere material comfort, is infected with endemic diseases which threaten to end humanity if not the human race. Husserl emphasized in his *Crisis of European Science and Humanity*[191] that nature as the experiential ground of man has in our time disappeared behind the intellectual constructions developed by science, and Romano Guardini in his *The End of Modern Times*,[192] has stressed the fact that by losing the sense of mystery and the sense of the unknown forces directing man and the universe, man's metaphysical perspective has greatly diminished, if not disappeared altogether. Merleau-Ponty has shown that the same kind of decay may be witnessed at the social level. In his *Phénoménologie de la perception*[193] he elaborates the point that the gregarious life of industrial civilization does not promote deeper human relations. On the contrary, social life is pursued at its most superficial standardized level, while man as an individual is cut off from his fellow man and remains isolated within the bounds of his inner life.

It would be difficult to establish when this erosion of man began in Western civilization; doubtless historians of culture and sociologists will probe deeper into its sources. However, from the philosophical point of view it seems clear that from the beginning of modern times, the experience of nature has been assumed to be the privileged, indeed the only valid, type of experience, and nature was construed as fundamentally "exterior" to man. In this way the initial approach to experience was fundamentally biased, for the validity of the experience of nature was supposed to consist in its revelation of what is essentially heterogeneous and alien to man. Furthermore, the nineteenth-century scientific outlook discredited the validity of all types of experience other than the sensory perception of nature under intellectually construed conditions. It seems that from these two main presuppositions stems the fact that modern science lost its human significance.

Our inquiry into the relation between phenomenological philosophy and science has led to the contrary view that, beneath all abstract differentiations, nature, man, and *Transcendence* are, at the initial point of man's emergence from the purely organic level into the meaningfulness of the world, but three dimensions of one scheme of the universe. We have seen how the phenomenological orientation generated not only techniques, but also a pattern for the investigation of structures, both of which have enabled science to reveal and corroborate that basic scheme. It became a novel ground for experience, a ground where the matter of revealing the essentially nonhuman was replaced by considering what experience can disclose of the unfathomable depths of man's universe, where nature on the one side and *Transcendence* on the other meet and necessitate each other. By the same process which led to the re-evaluation of science, the universal pattern of scientific inquiry has also become transformed and enlarged. It is now possible for the sciences to explore the various types of experience in all realms covering that ground. The results thereby obtained will not be used merely to improve the material conditions of man's existence on earth; they will be interpreted in the perspective of what they contribute toward the recognition of man's condition, and the novel light they shed on the way in which man's life can be transformed into a more authentic realization in the tension toward the metaphysical absolute. Thus science ceases to be merely a tool, for it can now acquire significance for man's essentially human, individual life.

We will now interpret the results of our entire study (1) from the point of view of the new sources of experience discerned and explored in outline, then (2) from the point of view of the new pattern of scientific investigation outlined. In other words, we shall first examine the concept of a universe which has ceased to be strange and brutal but has become instead a congenial locus for man. We will follow this with a review of the transformations in the basic foundations of scientific investigations, which have come about as a result of science's response to the new perspective of the universe which science itself discovered.

In our last chapter the "anthropological" conception of man within the phenomenological perspective has related him fundamentally to nature—not, however, by reducing man along the physicalistic lines of positivistic science but, on the contrary, by "humanizing" nature itself. Man, essentially defined by his *being-in-the-world,* sees himself and nature, in virtue of the constitutive power of his intentional consciousness, interwoven within one system of meanings. The world is shown to have the same spatio-temporal axis as man's psychic life and this axis, prior to the physicalistic constructions of science, refers to intentionality conceived as underlying both the laws of the world and those of the mind.

Thus the dichotomy of the immaterial mind and the extended body, of man and nature, has vanished. Man in his entirety is constituted with reference to the laws of the world, which laws express man's basic concerns. Nature is revealed, neither as a construct of experimental science nor as a brute physical background, but as essentially meaningful for individual human life. Commenting on Plato's *Timaeus*, A. E. Taylor has said, "In the real world there is always, over and above 'law' a factor of the 'simply given' or 'brute fact,' not accounted for and to be accepted simply as given." [194] If the realm of "law" is identified with the constitutive intentional structure of the world and the universe conceived as exemplifying the intelligible, meaningful aspect of nature, then its limits are extended to the point where any 'brute' nucleus falls beyond the scope and interest of man and science. On the contrary, a common ground supports both nature and man's primary being; only an abstract distinction of reason can distinguish them.

Instead of regarding the experience of nature as a search for elements extraneous to man which are therefore meaningless for his personal plan of life, psychology and psychopathology show sources of experience in which nature is amalgamated with man's basic receptivity, drives, and stimuli in the forms of images and myths. The purely emotional is intelligibly organized and thus acquires human significance. The forms assumed by the individual worlds, in which the lives of individuals are caught, express the innermost forms of their psychic and mental constitution. Therefore, as therapy in psychopathology has confirmed through the discovery of archetypes of emotions, we find a genuine source of experience in which, beneath the mechanized and distorted responses of contemporary man, an *authentic* intercourse between man and nature can be re-established and man's natural roots regenerated.

In this new orientation of man and nature it is the spiritual or *existential* dimension in man, developed into a meta-physical perspective of *Transcendence,* which plays a prominent role. We have seen how the dynamic conception of man, which understands him as the locus of self-creative tensions which are nevertheless basically oriented toward others, integrates the natural, the existential or spiritual, and the metaphysical in a dialectic of tensions mobilizing all human resources. In the resultant drive toward self-mastery there arises a new meaning of morality and of human freedom. Self-mastery, at the existential level, is in the first place the integration of the categories which in traditional philosophy have been treated as mutually exclusive. *Being,* traditionally opposed to *becoming* as the static is opposed to the dynamic, appears as the indispensable but transient fixation of stages. Essentialistic rational knowledge does not exclude the transcendent and nonrational; on the contrary, it is an indispensable tool which, by making analysis, recognition, reflection, and choice of provisory forms possible, works out the process of self-realization of the ego toward its transcendent *telos.* As in Leibniz, there would be no freedom without choice directed by rational recognition of alternatives.

In the essential perspective of nature-transcending tension, the other man cannot be conceived as an impartial spectator, but as man's perpetual point of reference in every function, culminating in the spiritual (existential) encounter, which must be met with unreserved, uncompromising sincerity, since the other man is a point of reference for one's own accomplishments. Man's freedom is basically *responsibility* for his realization; this responsibility is, however, not only to himself for his own strict individuality but to all men. Sartre remarks justly that when each man chooses himself, he simultaneously chooses for all men.[195] Each of our actions, creating us the man we want to be, creates at the same time an image of what we judge *all* men should be.

The moral life is a movement toward an *authentic* realization of the ego, based on genuine experience. But since man, in all his constitutive processes, is essentially linked with his fellows, no genuine experience of the self is possible except in relation to genuine experience of others.

In searching for a genuine experience of the other man, we have to leave behind all social conceptions for the sake of uncovering the genuine stand of man toward the world, life, and the absolute, for in this way may be found the source from which arise, underneath the mechanized responses of social man, the links of one man to another in their innermost nature. The basis for the new, authentic nature of human relations consists in sincerity without reserve, and in the will to communicate and share with others the deepest sense of life and love. When genuine experience with the other man is adopted as the focal point of one's own human horizon, the concepts of family, tradition, posterity, the continuity of cultural heritage and man's common share in it take on a fresh meaning for contemporary man and the man of the future, who, in striving to free himself from all traditional ties, has abandoned the ancient views. A basis is established for a new type of human solidarity, and with new meaning given to social forms, the individual is shown a way out of his isolation in contemporary mass society.

This new relation to the other man within the described framework is already conceived within a new metaphysical perspective: a perspective which constitutes a source of experience in which all man's concerns, his life and his destiny, may be illuminated at a higher and more complete level. Thus the possibility of salutary metaphysical wonder is reinstated.

These apparently "esoteric" aspects of man and the universe have been acknowledged to be more than mere metaphysical speculation: they are, rather, philosophical interpretations of some of the basic facts produced by scientific research, the elements of which have been discussed at length in the present study. It remains to be shown how the philosophical insights gained from science have also enriched the purely methodological aspect of phenomenological trends of thought.

As we have pointed out, the Cartesian postulate of the continuity of the universe with respect to extended substance has been replaced by the concept of a *many-layered* reality. Corresponding to the integration of several heterogeneous layers of reality within one structure, we have noticed four types of cognition and four corresponding methods of inquiry harmoniously incorporated within the universal methodological pattern of inquiry. Directed by (1) the purely descriptive aspect of phenomenological technique, that offering essential insight into structures; (2) the empirical method found its level of application; (3) deductive mathematical formulation appeared as the proper tool for the final formulation of results; and (4) the immediate experience of the self, the other man, and the human world was acknowledged as indispensable in various scientific fields.

Three criteria of truth, or rather of cognitive adequacy are recognized as compatible: (1) at the level of objective essentialistic cognition, the "objective" Aristotelian truth understood as the coordination of the ideas, or cognitive contents with objects of cognition; (2) the semantic conception of the systematic consistency of rational, "objective" structures; and (3) constitutive "authenticity" as applied to cognitive insights into the other man, and into the process of one's own becoming, with reference to both the simultaneous constitutive genesis of the ego within the world, and the poly-dimensionality of human nature.

This new methodological scheme obviously expresses the

specific type of collaboration of philosophy and the phenomenological sciences. This our basic theme, may be summarized by the following remarks of A. de Waelhens:

> These relations [between the sciences and philoso-
> phy] consist neither in subordination nor in simple
> coexistence. The philosopher's task is to make explicit
> the ontological status of human existent as that status
> is manifested in actual existence. But this task is pos-
> sible only by examining the facts which constitute
> that existence, i.e. with the collaboration of the scien-
> tist. On the other hand the scientist can seek and
> understand the facts only on the basis of a conception
> of man's being which alone enables him to determine
> what to look for and what dimension of intelligibility
> may properly be applied to the object of his research.
>
> It is too clear that these relations form a circle.
> Here again one finds the circle of existence itself,
> which cannot be understood without being, nor be
> without being understood.[196]

NOTES

1 Marvin Farber, *The Foundation of Phenomenology* (Harvard University Press, Cambridge, Mass.), p. 193.

2 See H. Feigl, *Logical Empiricism*, D. D. Runes, ed. (Philosophical Library, New York, 1943).

3 Edmund Husserl, *Ideas: General Introduction to Pure Phenomenology,* trans. by W. R. Boyce Gibson (Macmillan, New York, 1952), p. 55.

4 In German, *der Originär gebende Akt;* Boyce Gibson translates this somewhat artificially as "primordial dator act."

5 *Ibid.*, p. 92 (italics added).

6 Edmund Husserl, *Logische Untersuchungen* (Niemeyer, Halle, 1900-1901), vols. I, II.

7 For the technical aspect of phenomenological reduction see Marvin Farber's quoted book (Note 1), and F. P. Welch, *Edmund Husserl's Phenomenology* (Univ. So. Calif. Press, Los Angeles, 1939). Interpreting the basic ideas of phenomenology, we shall rely chiefly on Husserl's early writings, which were at the time pioneering. His posthumous work *Die Phänomenologie und die Fundamente der Wissenschaften, Husserliana* (Martinus Nijhoff, The Hague, 1952), Vol. III, does not introduce major changes.

8 Husserl's phenomenology has been carefully discussed in a great number of essays, articles and books from different points of view in several languages, English included. We limit ourselves to developing its relation to empirical cognition in respect to its rôle as the foundation of sciences intending to reestablish a universal and apodeictic science. Therefore we abandon specula-

tive interest of such a discussion for the sake of showing how phenomenological principles could have appeared relevant to empirical scientists.

9 Throughout this essay the terms "natural," "naturalistic," and "nature" will—unless otherwise specified—be used to denote the aspects of the world, man, and cognition as exhibited in sensory experience, pre-theoretically, without any reference to the "naturalistic" philosophy.

10 In his *Logische Untersuchungen,* Husserl has devoted extensive studies to establishing the specific nature of categorical vs. empirical perception, of which Farber's quoted essay gives a conscientious account. In the *Ideen zur reinen Phänomenologie* (1st ed. in *Jahrbuch für Philosophie und Phänomenologische Forschung,* 1913), he attempts to relate the rational content of categorical perception to the empirical one (material) within the nature of perception itself. The primordial assumption of the essential activity of intentional consciousness, however, prevents any explanation of how the empirical (material, passive) could be "imported" into the intentional act which lacks all passive receptivity. Therefore at this level of research Husserl is led toward transcendental idealism. Throughout his vast inquiries following *Ideen,* he nevertheless is attempting at various levels, as for example at the level of the genesis of logical forms, or at that of the constitution of the lifeworld (*Lebenswelt*) to which his extensive posthumous work is devoted (Vol. II, III, V, etc., of *Husserliana*), to establish an explanation of the continuity between the empirical and the eidetic realm within perception.

11 Cf. Emil Bréhier, *Les Thèmes Actuels de la Philosophie* (Paris, 1954).

12 Husserl himself made an extensive study of the phenomenological foundations of logic and arithmetic which has exercised a great influence upon contemporary research in these fields. Next to his fundamental work, *Logische Untersuchungen,* he has obtained particularly interesting results in his study, *Erfahrung und Urteil,* edited by Ludwig Landgrebe (Prague, 1939), and *Formale und Transzendentale Logic,* in *Jahrbuch for Philosophie und Phänomenologische Forschung* (Halle, 1929). He was directly followed by Oscar Becker and Alexander Pfänder. Oscar Becker first worked on the phenomenological foundations of geometry; more recently he has published a long essay on the foundations of mathematics. Cf. Oscar Becker, *Mathematische Existenz, Untersuchungen zur Logik und Ontologie mathematischer Phänomene, Jahrbuch* 1927, and *Grundlagen der Mathematik in geschichtlicher Entwicklung* (Freiburg, K. Albert, 1954). He and Pfänder have also worked on the foundations of logic, cf. Alexander Pfänder, *Logik,* in *Jahrbuch,* 1921; Oscar Pfänder, *Zur Logik der Modalitäten, Jahrbuch,* 1930.

13 The term "model" denotes in traditional use a prototype to be imitated by its "copies" (e.g., the model of a painter). In contemporary mathematical and empirical research it denotes theoretically constructed patterns, conceived beforehand, which serve as a tool for inquiry (e.g., testing patterns used in psychology). It is in this restricted methodological sense that we are using the term in this essay.

14 The present essay is intended as an interpretive picture of the philosophical basis of contemporary Continental thought rather than as a purely historical survey. Therefore, for the sake of the argument, we shall organize the presentation of different new insights, theories and developments in philosophy and science according to their place and significance in the over-all philosophical picture, often disregarding the historical chronology.

15 Nicolai Hartmann, *Die Anfänge des Schichtungsgedanken in der Alten Philosophie* (De Gruyter, Berlin, 1943), p. 3.

16 Max Scheler, *Der Formalismus in der Ethik und die Materiale Werthetik,* first ed. 1916; last ed. Franke, Bern, 1954. In psychology and psychiatry the layers theory was used by Joseph Froebes (*Lehrbuch der experimentalen Psychologie,* München, 3rd ed. 1929), Johannes Lindworsky (*Experimentale Psychologie,* München, 1921), Hendrik Rühmke, *Phänomenologische en Klinisch-psychiatrische Studie over het geluksgevoel* (Leiden, 1923. In the present essay we shall, however, concentrate on its application in other realms of inquiry.
For Scheler's conception of layers cf. infra p. 62.

17 Roman Ingarden, *Das Literarische Kunstwerk* (Niemeyer, Halle, 1931).

18 Cf. P. Leon, Critical note on Ingarden's *Das Literarische Kunstwerk,* in *Mind,* Vol. XLI, 1931.

19 *Ibid.*

20 *Ibid.,* p. 24.

21 *Ibid.,* pp. 29-53.

22 Cf. *Das Literarische Kunstwerk,* pp. 293-297.

23 Cf. *ibid.,* pp. 185-278.

24 *Ibid.,* pp. 293-297.

25 *Ibid.,* pp. 384-389.

26 *Ibid.,* p. 384.

27 *Ibid.,* p. 385.

28 Nicolai Hartmann, *Das Problem des Geistigen Seins* (de Gruyter, Berlin, 1933), p. 376.

29 René Wellek and Austin Warren, *Theory of Literature* (Harcourt, New York, 1949), pp. 152-158.

30 *Ibid.,* pp. 158-159 and pp. 235-249.

31 Cf. *Philosophical Thought in France and in the United States,* Buffalo, 1950. Jean Hering in his account of phenomenology in France emphasizes the phenomenological approach to historical inquiry as introduced by Alexandre Koyré in his essay on Galileo. The crucial problem of methodology in historical science consists in the uncertainty not only about the occurrence of historical events but also about their nature; since historical statements are supported by differently oriented and informed, sometimes even contradictory, testimonies, the final question facing every sound historical inquiry is, if not the question: "Has the event factually occurred?" at least the question: "What was it really like?"
Koyré, applying the phenomenological method, considers historical events and their features, as well as the historical context in which they occur, in their essential "intrinsic," structure. The inherent uncertainty of statements concerning factual events and their nature ceases to be a matter of controversy between partisans of different source material since the essential structure discovered in some crucial documentary data determines which other data are credible and which are to be excluded.

32 Mikel Dufrenne, *Phénoménologie de l'Objet Esthétique* (Paris, 1950).

33 André Malraux, *Psychologie de l'Art* (Skira, Geneva, 1947).

34 Cf. Hartmann's previously quoted *Das Problem des Geistigen Seins.*

35 *Ibid.,* pp. 419-447. As we have just mentioned, Hartmann extends Ingarden's theory of the literary work of art to all other works of the fine

arts. He transposes the four-strata theory analogically to all of them without making separate analyses for each art. He has amplified the same procedure in his *Aesthetik,* (Berlin, 1953). However, Ingarden pursuing *his* method of a minute analysis of other than literary works of art (for example a work of plastic art, a picture) arrives at a strata structure different than that of the literary work. Cf. *O budowie Obrazu* (Polska Akademia Nauk, Warszawa, 1946). This analysis of the picture was written in 1929 but published only after the war.

36 Hartmann, *Der Aufbau der realen Welt* (A. Hain, 1949).

37 Jean Piaget, *Psychologie de l'Intelligence* (Colin, Paris, 1947), pp. 1-10; or the same book published as *The Psychology of Intelligence,* trans, by Malcolm Piercy and D. E. Berlyne (Harcourt, New York, 1950).

38 *Ibid.,* p. 20, French edition.

39 Maurice Merleau-Ponty, *La Structure du Comportement* (Paris, 1948).

40 Claude Lévi-Strauss, *Les Structures Élémentaires de la Parenté* (Presses Universitaires de France, Paris, 1949).

41 *Ibid.,* pp. 278-285.

42 We have considered Sartre's and Merleau-Ponty's psychological studies apart from the widespread phenomenological trends in psychology because of their special relevance for our present methodological argument. We devote subsequent sections to the essential import of phenomenology for psychology.

43 Jean-Paul Sartre, *The Psychology of Imagination* (Philosophical Library, New York, 1948), p. 1.

44 *Ibid.,* p. 8.

45 *Ibid.,* p. 8.

46 *Ibid.,* p. 212.

47 By "descriptive psychology of understanding" we mean here Dilthey's *"Verstehende Psychologie."*

48 Paul Guillaume, *Psychologie de la Forme* (Paris, 1937), p. 147 (quoted also by Bréhier).

49 Jean Piaget, *Le dévéloppement de la notion du temps chez l'enfant* (Presses Univ., Paris, 1946), and other studies well known in the United States.

50 Erwin Straus, "The Sigh, An Introduction to a Theory of Expression," *Tijdschrift voor Philosophie* (1952), No. 9. The difference between Straus's study of *expression* and the research of the behaviorists with whom he shares the object of inquiry, structures of comportment, consists in the fact that Straus is analyzing the immediately perceivable structures of comportment while behavioral research is inquiring into its mechanism by inference. Furthermore Straus is limiting analysis of these structures to their simple description, without any reference to their foundation, while the conception and method of behavioral research relies on the assumption of the physical nature of the observed phenomenon.

51 W. Dilthey, *Ideen über eine Beschreibende und Zergliedernde Psychologie* (1924).

52 Cf. the account of the Würzburg school—however, not quite exact, and from a partisan point of view—given by E. Brunswik in "The Conceptual Framework of Psychology" in *The International Encyclopedia of Unified Science* (Univ. of Chicago Press, Chicago, 1955), Vol. I, Part II.

53 Max Scheler, *Zur Phänomenologie und Theorie der Sympathiegefühle und von Liebe und Hass; mit einem Anhang über den Grund zur Annahme*

der Existenz des Fremden Ich (Niemeyer, Halle, 1913). Max Scheler, *Die Transzendentale und die Psychologische Methode* (F. Meiner, Leipzig, 1922). A. Pfänder, *Die Seele des Menschen, Versuch einer Verstehenden Psychologie* (Niemeyer, Halle, 1933).

54 Particularly Jaspers' *Psychologie der Weltanschaungen* (Springer, Berlin, 1919), which has marked a turning point in contemporary psychiatry and psychopathology.

55 Cf. Ludwig Binswanger, "Lebensfunktion und innere Lebensgeschichte" in *Monatsschrift für Psychiatrie und Neurologie* (1928), No. 68.

56 Jaspers as a psychiatrist agrees with Scheler's distinction and Binswanger's interpretation of the *inner biography;* he has, as we shall see, given to it a philosophical foundation and background.

57 Cf. Max Scheler, "Liebe und Hass" in *Wesen und Formen der Sympathie* (Cohen, Bonn, 1931), pp. 2-8.

58 *Ibid.*, pp. 234-235.

59 E. Bleuler, *Textbook of Psychiatry*, trans. by A. A. Brill (Macmillan, New York, 1924).

60 By autism is meant the general mental isolation of the schizophrenic patient; his incommunicability.

61 As far as the nature of autism is concerned, Karl Jaspers' *Allgemeine Psychopathologie* (Springer, Berlin, 1913, revised 1953), and his studies on Strindberg and Van Gogh were fundamental.

62 E. Kretschmer, *Der Sensitive Beziehungswahn* (Springer, Berlin, 1918); H. C. Rühmke, *Zur Phänomenologie des Klinischen Glucksgefühls* (Springer, Berlin, 1920); van der Horst, *Anthropological Psychiatry* (Amsterdam, 1946); Gurdsdorf, *La Découverte de soi* (Presses Universitaires, Paris, 1948). For a more extensive bibliography see J. H. van den Berg, *The Phenomenological Approach to Psychiatry* (C. C. Thomas, Springfield, Ill., 1955).

63 Hedwig Conrad Martius, "Zur Phänomenologie und Erscheinunglehre der Realen Aussenwelt," in *Jahrbuch für Philosophie und Phänomenologische Forschung*, Vol. III, 1916.

64 Karl Jaspers, *Philosophie*, Vol. I (*Philosophische Weltorientierung*), *Philosophie*, Vol. II (*Existenzerhellung*) and Vol. III (Metaphysik) 2nd ed. 1948; *Von der Wahrheit* (*Philosophische Logik*), 1947, by T. Springer, Berlin.

65 Jaspers, *Philosophie*, Vol. I, Introduction.

66 Binswanger, "Uber die Daseins-Analytische Forschungs-Richtung in der Psychiatrie," in *Ausgewählte Vorträge und Aufsätze* (A. Franke, A.G., Bern, 1947).

67 It is the description of the patient's *de facto* attitude toward the world that Binswanger takes as fundamental, instead of the hypothetical, theoretically constructed, concept of libido. On the other hand, as we shall see (cf. *infra, supra*), what does this state mean if not a narrowness of the patient's *"Weltentwurf"*—"world projection"?

68 Cf. his capital work, *Allgemeine Psychopathologie*.

69 This is what Jaspers says in reply to the article by L. Lefebre, "The Psychology of Karl Jaspers," in *The Philosophy of Karl Jaspers* (Tudor, New York, 1957), edited by Paul A. Schilpp. We had the privilege of consulting the manuscript. Jaspers refers to his study in 1913, *Über die Grenzen der Psychologie*.

70 For an elaboration of Jaspers' approach at this point see the quoted essay by Lefebre (Note 69).

71 "Understanding" (*"Verstehen"*) differs from the "explanation" attempted by experimental methods in that the latter presupposes an empirically existing cause-to-effect relationship, while the relations to be treated by "understanding" are of a non-empirical nature. They are "meaningful" relations, whether between coexisting phenomena, as for example the patient's symptoms and his biographical data, or the development of these symptoms one after another. Jaspers conceives phenomenological "understanding" as "illustrative representation of individual experience."

72 Jaspers sees it also as a prerogative of mind to give to things logical determination with a rational pattern of connection, even though there is in his opinion no extra-mental unity of either beings or science.

73 Referring to this mode of being ("object" or *"Dasein"*) we shall use the term existence in the sense of everyday existence.

74 *Philosophie*, Vol. II, p. 255 of the German edition. All translations by the present writer.

75 Human *Dasein* corresponds to Kant's *empirical ego*, and is, like the latter, an *object* with respect to the mind and within the schemata of Kantian categories.

76 *Philosophie*, Vol. II, p. 255.

77 *Ibid.*, p. 1.

78 *Ibid.*, p. 1.

79 *Ibid.*, p. 1.

80 *Ibid.*, p. 17.

81 The possibility of a complete cognition of *Existenz* has, as we shall see in what follows, a quite particular meaning.

82 *Philosophie*, Vol. I, p. 40.

83 *Ibid.*, p. 40.

84 *Ibid.*, p. 51.

85 *Ibid.*, Vol. II, p. 119.

86 *Ibid.*, p. 119.

87 *Ibid.*, p. 257.

88 The spiritually "therapeutic" value of religious institutions like confession, for example, has long been recognized. On the other hand the extent of mental disturbance in contemporary society can be considered as a result of socially more developed but personally less profound and intimate kinds of human relations.

89 According to the psychologist Lefebre (cf. *infra*) Jaspers' contribution to a philosophically founded psychology, psychiatry and psychoanalysis (remaining, however, always an empirical science), beginning with the appearance of his *Allgemeine Psychopathologie* (cf. *infra*) and continuing with other studies, cannot be overestimated. He offers a systematically elaborated philosophical expression for philosophically based researches with the phenomenological method. His influence on psychiatrists such as L. Binswanger, Kuhn and Haeberlin in Switzerland; Strauss and Goldstein in the United States; Buytendijk in the Netherlands; Bachelard, E. Minkowski, and Le Senne in France, is noteworthy (for the bibliography see the above quoted J. H. van den Berg, *The Phenomenological Approach to Psychiatry*).

The fundamental points of Jaspers' philosophy—as for example the consideration of the main philosophical problems from the point of view of man understood in his totality; the complete content of human life seen in the light of self-realization; man's *ethos* seen in a higher form of the latter—

express the root or basic tendencies of several prominent philosophers such as G. Marcel, Louis Lavelle, Maurice Merleau-Ponty, etc., as well as of a humanistic trend in contemporary European literature, which has issued from their thought. On the other hand, Jaspers' distinctions concerning various ways of cognition, corresponding to the conception of the totality of human nature and its encompassing freedom, fall in line with the common ground of European contemporary thought, whether philosophical, artistic, scientific or cultural. Jaspers' metaphysical conception of God in terms of *Transcendence* and his proposed philosophical interpretation of the meaning of the spiritual life and the way towards human perfection in terms of *Existenz* and its elucidation meets, in its fundamental points, the new trends in Protestant theology issuing from the same source. This trend, inaugurated by Karl Barth, runs parallel to Jaspers' metaphysics; both refer back to Kierkegaard. Some of its followers, however, have been directly inspired by the thought of Jaspers and Heidegger, as, for example, the German theologians Rudolf Bultman and Paul Tillich who accept their philosophical ideas as a foundation for theological speculation. Cf. Bultman, *Theology of the New Testament* (Scribner's, New York, 1951); Tillich, *Systematic Theology* (Univ. of Chicago Press, Chicago, 1951); George W. Davis, *Existentialism and Theology* (Philosophical Library, New York, 1957).

90 Gabriel Marcel, *Journal Métaphysique* (Gallimard, Paris, 1927), pp. 62, 145. To use Jacques Paliard's expression commenting on Marcel "the relation of consciousness to consciousness is more real and more concrete than the consciousness itself."

91 Gabriel Marcel, *Homo Viator: Introduction to a Metaphysic of Hope*, trans. by Emma Craufurd (Gollancz, London, 1951), p. 13.

92 *Ibid.*, pp. 125-134.

93 *Ibid.*, pp. 68-97.

94 *Ibid.*, pp. 98-125.

95 Paul Claudel, *Art Poetic: Connaissance du Temps* (Mercure de France, Paris, 3rd ed., 1915), p. 69.

96 Maxime Chastaing, *La Connaissance d'Autrui* (Presses Universitaires, Paris).

97 Maurice Nédoncelle, *La Reciprocité des Consciences* (Aubier, Paris, 1942); *Vers une Philosophie de l'Amour* (Aubier, 1953).

98 Phenomenological clues in the approach to subject matter, in terms of stratified, structural, or irreducible phenomena, have pervaded contemporary sociology. It can be said in general that a new tendency has developed in America, paralleling the phenomenological attitude in Europe and in opposition to the evolutionary tradition, that considers the social in terms of a phenomenon which is irreducible to more elementary factors from which it could progressively develop. This tendency attempts to grasp the social by means of certain types of specific structures without regard for any economic, political, judicial, or religious content.

99 Georges Gurvitch, *Vocation Actuelle de la Sociology: Vers une Sociology Différentielle*, 1950.

100 Edmund Husserl, *Kartesianische Meditationen und Pariser Vorträge*, in *Husserliana*, S. Strasser, editor (Nijhoff, The Hague, 1950). See our section on Husserl and constitutive phenomenology.

101 A. Vierkant, *Gesellschaftslehre*, 2nd ed., 1928.

102 Theodor Litt, *Individuum und Gemeinschaft* (1926).

[103] Theodor Geiger, "Die Gruppe und die Kategorien Gemeinschaft und Gesellschaft" in *Vierteljahresschrift für Wissenschaftliche Philosophie und Sociologie* (Leipzig, 1927); also *Die Gestalten der Gesellung* (Karlsruhe, 1928).

[104] E. Durkheim, *Formes Élémentaires de la Vie Religieuse* (Alcan, Paris, 1925), pp. 22-23.

[105] E. Dupréel, *Sociologie Générale* (Presses Universitaires, Paris, 1948).

[106] George Gurvitch, *Essais d'une Classification Pluraliste des Formes de Sociabilité*, 1938, pp. 14, 16.

[107] Adolf Reinach, "Die Apriorischen Grundlagen des Bürgerlichen Rechts," in *Jahrbuch*, 1913. (Second edition, Kösel Verlag, Munich, 1955).

[108] *Ibid.*, cf. *Jahrbuch*, p. 693.

[109] *Ibid.*, p. 698.

[110] *Ibid.*, p. 707.

[111] *Ibid.*, p. 715.

[112] The legal notion of promise is characterized by the necessity of being addressed to someone and declared, while the moral (*sittlich*) notion of promise does not require this relation to the other person; it can be made to oneself and remain canceled.

[113] *Ibid.*, p. 715.

[114] By its leitmotif, this section belongs rather to Chapter I. We include it here, however, to form a general picture of the social sciences.

[115] F. A. Lutz, Introduction to Walter Eucken's *The Foundation of Economics; History and Theory in the Analysis of Economic Reality*, translated into English by T. W. Hutchison, (The Univ. of Chicago Press, Chicago, 1951), (first German ed. in 1940), p. 6.

[116] *Ibid.*, p. 7.

[117] *Ibid.*, p. 31.

[118] Othmar Spann, *Fundamente der Volkswirtschaftlehre* (Gustav Fischer Verlag, Jena, 1st. ed. 1917).

[119] Eucken's previously cited book (note 115), p. 52.

[120] *Ibid.*, p. 116.

[121] *Ibid.*, p. 118.

[122] *Ibid.*, p. 118.

[123] *Ibid.*, p. 118.

[124] *Ibid.*, p. 118.

[125] *Ibid.*, p. 130.

[126] *Ibid.*, p. 130.

[127] *Ibid.*, p. 300.

[128] *Ibid.*, p. 300.

[129] *Ibid.*, p. 300.

[130] Cf. Albert Saloman, "German Sociology," in *Twentieth Century Sociology*, edited by George Gurvitch and Wilbert E. Moore (The Philosophical Library, New York, 1945), p. 612.

[131] We refer here to the previously quoted *Cartesian Meditations*, but especially to *Ideas II, Ideas III*, and the *Krisis der Europäischen Wissenschaften und die transzendentale Phänomenologie*, which have been published only recently. Except for a fragment of the *Krisis*, these late writings of Husserl remained for a long time in manuscript form only. Therefore the further developments of Husserl's phenomenology become the center of attention only in the most recent times. Cf. Anna-Teresa Tymieniecka:

"Quelques Remarques sur l'État Actuel de la Phénoménologie," in *Annales Universitatis Saraviensis*, Vol. V, *Philosophie*, 1954.

132 Alfred Schütz, "Phenomenology and Social Sciences," in *Philosophical Essays in Memory of Edmund Husserl* (Harvard University Press, Cambridge, 1940), pp. 165-186.

133 Cf. Edmund Husserl, *Krisis der Europäischen Wissenschaften und die transzendentale Phänomenologie* (The Hague, Martinus Nijhoff, 1954).

134 Cf. Anna-Teresa Tymieniecka, above, note 131.

135 We limit ourselves here to merely mentioning these problems in anticipation of their treatment in the next part of our study. It is interesting to see that the main themes of contemporary philosophy which, as developed by Husserl's followers, came to a prominent position, were already pointed out and treated by Husserl himself.

136 Cf. Schütz's quoted essay and his study: *Das Problem der Transzendentalen Intersubjectivität bei Husserl, Colloque de Royaumont sur l'Oeuvre et la Pensée de Husserl*, 1957.

137 Cf. Schütz's *Phenomenology and the Social Sciences*, p. 180.

138 Alfred Schütz, *Der Sinnhafte Aufbau der Sozialen Welt* (Vienna, 1932).

139 Cf. *Phenomenology and the Social Sciences*, p. 181.

140 *Ibid.*, p. 181.

141 *Ibid.*, p. 183.

142 Cf. Alfred Stonier and Karl Bode, "A New Approach to the Methodology of Social Sciences," in *Economica*, IV, Nov., 1937, pp. 406-427.

143 Martin Heidegger, *Was ist Metaphysik* (Klostermann Verlag, 1930).

144 Cf. *Theoretical Biology*, v. Uexküll, English translation by D. L. Maccinnon (Harcourt, New York, 1926), p. 126: "Every animal is a subject, which . . . in virtue of the structure peculiar to it, selects stimuli from the general influences of the outer world, and to these it responds in a certain way. These responses, in their turn, consist of certain effects on the outer world, and these again influence the stimuli. In this way there arises a self-contained periodic cycle, which we may call the *function-circle* of the animal. . . . The sum of the stimuli affecting an animal forms a world in itself. The stimuli, considered in connection with the *function-circle* as a whole, form certain indications, which enable the animal to guide its movements, much as the signs at sea enable the sailor to steer his ship. I call the sum of the indications the *world-as-sensed*." Cf. also p. 59, footnote 66.

145 *Ibid.* "The animal itself, by the very fact of exercising such direction (see previous footnote), creates a world for itself, which I shall call the *inner world*." Also later Weizsäcker in his *Gestaltkreis. Theorie der Einhet von Wahrnehmung und Bewegung*, 1940, overcomes the classical opposition of subject and object.

146 Cf. I. v. Uexküll, *Umwelt und Innenwelt der Tiere* (Springer, Berlin, 1909).

147 *Niegeschauten Welten; Die Umwelten Meiner Freunde.*

148 We take this example from L. Binswanger's article, "Über die Daseinsanalytische Forschungsrichtung in der Psychiatrie," p. 198, in *Ausgewählte Vorträge und Aufsätze* (Franke A. G., Bern, 1947).

149 The term *"Dasein"* is used by Heidegger in a different sense than by Jaspers, for whom it denotes a "natural" being, an "object," "everyday existence."

194 | Notes

150 Cf. *Sein und Zeit*, p. 9, I. ed., in *Jahrbuch* (Halle, 1927).

151 Heidegger's concept of *"Sorge"* is usually translated into English by the term "care." In order to avoid the common misinterpretations of this fundamental conception, I introduce the term "concern," "to be concerned with" (besought). I feel that the translation of *Sorge* by "care" stems from the widespread misinterpretation of Heidegger's philosophy in psychological terms. The present paper's intention is to re-establish its original meaning in terms of fundamental intentionality.

152 *Ibid.*, p. 26.

153 Cf. *Sein und Zeit*, pp. 318-321.

154 *Ibid.*, p. 322.

155 The current philosophical understanding confuses the self-hood with the closed psychological subject; by this permanency would be meant the persistence of the identity of the subject as a substance.

156 Talking about the physicality of the world and man (nature) in terms of the "brute reality," Heidegger denies neither their existence nor their validity; he considers it only as one of the aspects of human universe, and in respect to intentionality not the fundamental one, but constructed upon it as its ground.

157 *Sein und Zeit*, p. 111.

158 *Ibid.*, p. 369.

159 Cf. Yvonne Pickard, *La Notion du Temps Chez Husserl et Heidegger*, No. 1, *Cahiers de Philosophie*, (Deucalion, Paris, 1946-47).

160 *Sein und Zeit*, p. 324.

161 *Ibid.*, p. 365.

162 *Ibid.*, p. 366. We have intended to clarify the popular misunderstanding of interpreting Heidegger's thought—on its shallow surface—as "subjectivisme."

163 Heidegger's conception of the world gave a new orientation to European philosophy and science. In its light, Merleau-Ponty is reinterpreting the psychology of behavior (*La structure du comportement* [Paris, 1945]). Showing first the fundamental difference between human behavior as involving sequences of symbols in opposition to the merely mechanical behavior of animals, he shows—opposing the interpretation of Watson, which leads to admitting only one physical substance—how far the structures of behavior reveal man's integration in a meaningful world by physical means. Stimulated both by Heidegger's conception of man as being-in-the-world as well as by the last works of Husserl concerning the structures of the world of the pre-theoretical life, the problems of epistemology are treated in this framework as problems of "constitution" of the lived-world. European anthropology is evolving in a similar direction. See, for instance, Paul Häberlin (*Der Mensch*, Zurich, 1941).

164 Ludwig Binswanger, *Über die Daseinsanalytische Forschungsrichtung in der Psychiatrie, Schweizerische Archiv für Psychologie und Neurologie*, 57, H. 2, 1946.

165 Binswanger refers to Goldstein's *Der Aufbau des Organismus*, 1934, who, introducing into biological research the world concept, makes a methodological principle that a defective organism can achieve an organized functioning only by a corresponding adjustment with its milieu.

166 Ludwig Binswanger, "Gescheinis und Erlebnis," p. 80, *Monatschrift für Psychiatrie*, 1931.

167 Binswanger has taken this case from the *Jahrbuch Bleuler und Freud*, III.

168 For another typical clinical application of the world project conception see Roland Kuhn, "Daseinsanalyse eines Falles von Schizophrenie," *Monatschrift für Psychiatrie und Neurologie*, Vol. 112, Nr. 5/6. In the field of schizophrenia further particularly important contributions have been made by E. Minkowski. To illustrate how appreciated is his scholarship by practitioners, we may evoke the thanks expressed to him officially by an Argentinian philosopher on behalf of mentally ill people from Argentina "for all he has done for them" at the XI International Congress for Philosophy in Brussels, 1933, an unusual and unrecorded event. In particular reference to the aspects of intentional anthropology in the present paper, the following should be quoted: Franz Fischer, "Zeitstruktur und Schizophrenie," *Zeitschrift für die gesammte Neurologie und Psychiatrie*, 121, 1929, and Franz Fischer, *Über die Wandlungen des Raumes im Aufbau des Schizophrenen Erlebniswelt, Nervenarzt*, 7, 1934. For further bibliography see the above quoted book of van den Berg.

169 Eugene Minkowski, *Le Temps Vécu, Etudes Phénoménologiques et Psychopathologiques* (Paris, 1933).

170 *Le Temps Vécu*, p. 16.

171 A similar conception was expressed by Pierre Janet, in his *L'évolution de la Mémoire et de la Notion du Temps* (Malaine, Paris, 1928), to which Minkowski refers.

172 E. Minkowski, *Le Temps Vécu*, pp. 3-4.

173 *Le temps vécu*, p. 169.

174 Gaston Bachelard, *La Psychoanalyse de Feu* (Gallimard, Paris, 1949), p. 215.

175 G. Bachelard, *La Terre et les Rêvéries la Volonté* (Jose Corti, Paris, 1948), p. 3.

176 C. G. Jung, *L'inconscient de la Vie Psychique normale et Anormale* (Paris, 1928), p. 110, quoted also by Désoille.

177 Henri Bergson, *L'energie Spirituelle*.

178 G. Bachelard, *La Terre et les Rêvéries de la Volonté*, p. 8.

179 H. Steffers, *Was ich Erlebte* (Breslau, 1840).

180 Robert Desoille, 1.) *Exploration de l'Affectivité Subconsciente par la Méthode du Rêve Éveillé—Sublimation et acquisitions psychologiques*, (Artrey, Paris, 1938; 2.) *Le Rêve Éveillé en Psychothérapie* (Presses Universitaires, Paris, 1945).

181 Cf. *infra*.

182 Jean-Paul Sartre, *L'Etre et le Néant, Essai d'Ontologie Phenomenologique*, (Paris, NRF, 1948), pp. 84-111; translated into English by Hazel E. Barnes: *Being and Nothingness, An Essay on Phenomenological Ontology* (Philosophical Library, New York, 1956).

183 *Ibid.*, pp. 104-105.

184 *Ibid.*, p. 644.

185 Sartre criticizes here a work by Paul Bourget, *Essai de Psychologie Contemporaine*: G. Flaubert (Plon-Nourrit, Paris, 1917).

186 *Ibid.*, p. 651.

187 *Ibid.*, p. 652.

188 Alfred Stern, *Sartre's Philosophy and Psychoanalysis* (Philosophical Library, New York, 1954).

189 Sartre, *L'Etre et le Néant,* p. 653.

190 Oswald Spengler, *Der Untergang des Abendlandes; Umriss einer Morphologie der Weltgeschichte* (Beck, München, 1922-23).

191 E. Husserl, *Die Krisis der Europäischen Wissenschaften und die transzendentale Phänomenologie, Husserliana* (The Hague, 1954). A fragment of this work under the title, *Die Krisis der Europäschen Wissenschaften und des Europäischen Menschentums,* has first appeared in the Journal *Philosophia* (Belgrade, 1836).

192 Romano Guardini, *Das Ende der Neuzeit: ein Versuch zur Orientierung,* 3rd ed. (Wurzburg, 1951).

193 Maurice Merleau-Ponty, *Phénomenologie de la Perception* (PUF, Paris, 1947).

194 Quoted by A. N. Whitehead, in *Process and Reality,* p. 67.

195 Jean-Paul Sartre, *L'Existentialisme est un Humanisme* (Nagel, Paris, 1951), p. 25.

196 Alfons de Waelhens, *Existence et Signification,* E. Nauuelaerts, 1958; essay: *Sciences Humaines, Horizons ontologiques et Rencontre,* p. 26.

INDEX